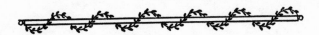

NEW ESSAYS

BY

OLIVER GOLDSMITH

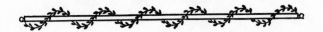

NEW ESSAYS

BY

OLIVER GOLDSMITH

NOW FIRST COLLECTED
AND EDITED
WITH AN INTRODUCTION AND NOTES

By

RONALD S. CRANE

GREENWOOD PRESS, PUBLISHERS
NEW YORK

To

J. F. C.

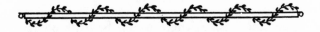

PREFACE

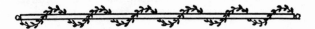

THE eighteen essays printed in this volume appeared originally, between January, 1760 and June, 1762, as anonymous contributions to the *British Magazine*, the *Royal Magazine*, the *Public Ledger*, the *Lady's Magazine*, and *Lloyd's Evening Post*. So far as I am aware, they are here for the first time ascribed to Oliver Goldsmith.

In reprinting them I have taken all reasonable pains to insure a literally faithful text. I have, however, in the interest of typographical uniformity, normalized the use of quotation marks, and I have added titles, with a precautionary note, whenever these were lacking in the originals.

The notes which accompany the text are intended primarily to supplement the Introduction by furnishing the detailed evidence upon which my ascriptions of the essays to Goldsmith are founded. Only on a few points is information given of a purely explanatory sort: anything like a full historical commentary would only confuse the issue for the reader of this volume, and besides there would be little point in anticipating the critical edition of Goldsmith's works which is now in preparation and in which these essays, if their authenticity is accepted, will naturally find a place. Within the limits of this special purpose, however, I have attempted to give enough material, in the way of parallel texts and references, to permit the reader to form his own judgment without undue inconvenience. In particular, I have made a practice of quoting parallel passages in full whenever the exact thought or language seemed in any way significant and of reproducing the original form of a text whenever the form given in the latest collected edition of Goldsmith[1] represented a subsequent revision by the author or seemed open to the suspicion of corruption.

For assistance in the preparation of the text and notes I am chiefly indebted to my wife. I have also received valuable help on particular points from Mrs. G. R. Osler, Mr. Herbert K. Stone, Professor F. B. Kaye, Professor George T. Northup, and Professor Henry W. Prescott.

R. S. C.

CHICAGO, ILLINOIS
November 10, 1927

[1] *The Works of Oliver Goldsmith*, edited by J. W. M. Gibbs, London, 1885–86. 5 vols. The references in the Introduction and notes to *Works* are to be understood as applying to this edition.

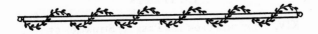

CONTENTS

INTRODUCTION

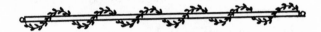

I

THAT even at this late date additions to the accepted canon of Goldsmith's essays are still possible need not surprise us if we consider the manner in which this canon has been formed. A beginning was made in Goldsmith's lifetime with the three collections which either bore his name or were known by contemporaries to be his—the *Bee* (1759), the *Citizen of the World* (1762), and *Essays by Mr. Goldsmith* (1765), the last, in its definitive form (1766), containing twenty-seven prose essays, of which all but ten, however, had already found a place in one or another of the two earlier collections. Although it must have been apparent to many that the pieces included in these volumes represented only a selection of Goldsmith's miscellaneous writings for periodicals, no noteworthy attempt was made to add to their number until over two decades after his death.[1] Then at the beginning

[1] I have noted but six new ascriptions before 1798. In 1772 a collection entitled *The Beauties of the Magazines, and Other Periodical Works* .... (2 vols.; London: Richardson and Urquhart) republished eleven

of 1798 appeared anonymously, published by J. Johnson, a collection entitled *Essays and Criticisms by Dr. Goldsmith*, the second and third volumes of which brought together fifty-one pieces, essays and reviews, only fourteen of which had previously been ascribed to Goldsmith.[1] Of the thirty-seven new pieces, twenty-five were taken from the *British Magazine*, ten from the *Critical Review*, and two from the *Westminster Magazine*, though in no case was there any indication of source.[2] Who was responsible

essays by Goldsmith; but though the announcement on the title-page that "None of these Pieces are to be found in the Works that pass under the Names of the above Authors" [Colman, Goldsmith, Murphy, Smollett, and Thornton] may have been literally true, the two volumes contained only one piece ascribed to Goldsmith that had not already appeared in either the *Bee* or the *Citizen of the World*, and that was "An Essay on the Animal World" extracted from R. Brookes's *New and Accurate System of Natural History* (1763). In April, 1774, the *Universal Magazine* (LIV, 171–72) printed an "Essay on Friendship, written by the late Dr. Oliver Goldsmith (never published in his works)"; this was later added to the acknowledged essays in *The Miscellaneous Works of Oliver Goldsmith* (London: W. Griffin, 1775; reprinted in 1786). In 1780 a volume called *Novellettes, Selected for the Use of Young Ladies and Gentlemen; Written by Dr. Goldsmith, Mrs. Griffiths, &c.*, contained reprints of two pieces originally published in the *Westminster Magazine* for February, 1773—"A Register of Scotch Marriages" and "The History of Cyrillo Padovano, the Noted Sleep-Walker" (see Iolo A. Williams, *Seven XVIIIth Century Bibliographies* [London, 1924], p. 175). In October, 1785, the *European Magazine* (VIII, 247–48) reprinted two papers— "The History of Carolan" and "On the Different Schools of Music"— from the *British Magazine* for 1760, marking them both "written by Dr. Goldsmith."

[1] I have used the British Museum copy, which differs bibliographically in several particulars from that described by J. W. M. Gibbs (*Works of Oliver Goldsmith*, V [1886], 412–14).

[2] The provenience of all but one of the essays was traced by Gibbs (*op. cit.*, V, 412–13). This one, a paper on "Filial Ingratitude," appeared originally in the *British Magazine*, I (September, 1760), 532–36.

for the collection in its final form has never been satisfactorily determined,[1] but a prefatory note at the beginning of Volume II undertook to reassure the public as to the authority of the selection:

> . . . . though the ESSAYS, published by Dr. GOLD-SMITH himself, were received by the world as the genuine efforts of genius, they were still but a selection. Many pieces of undoubted excellence were known to be omitted, and some which were suspected to be of his composition could not be certainly ascertained. These circumstances occasioned enquiry, and enquiry was the means of bringing to light what otherwise would not have been known. The late Mr. THOMAS WRIGHT, Printer, a man of literary observation and experience, had, during his connection with those periodical publications, in which the early works of Dr. GOLDSMITH were originally contained, carefully marked the several compositions of the different writers, as they were delivered to him to print. Being therefore, it was supposed, the only person able to separate the genuine performances of Dr. GOLDSMITH from those of other writers, in these miscellaneous collections, it became the wish of several admirers of the Author of The Traveller and Deserted Village, that his authentic writings should no longer be blended with either doubtful or spurious pieces. Mr. WRIGHT was therefore recommended and prevailed upon to print the present Selection, which he had just compleated at the time of his death.[2]

This would seem to be sufficiently explicit. Unfortunately, it is hard to feel satisfied that the statement really means all it appears to mean; for, though we can be fairly certain that Wright

---

[1] See Gibbs, *op. cit.*, V, 413–14.

[2] II, vii–ix.

had printed the *Critical Review* and the *Westminster Magazine*,[1] there is no definite evidence, so far as I know, that he had had anything to do with the *British Magazine*, from which the great majority of the new essays in Johnson's collection were taken. A good many of the essays reprinted from this periodical certainly exhibit no evident traces of Goldsmith's manner or ideas, and some of them—the "Belles-Lettres" series, for example, which was here for the first time injected into the canon—are, I believe, demonstrably not by Goldsmith.[2] Whatever may have been the contents of Wright's list, moreover, it was not the only source on which the compiler or compilers of the collection relied: the last ten essays in Volume III were almost certainly taken from a miscellaneous compilation, *The Beauties of the Magazines, and Other Periodical Works*, published in 1772.[3] In short, when examined closely, this first ambitious attempt to enlarge the canon of Goldsmith's periodical writing

[1] See Nichols, *Literary Anecdotes of the Eighteenth Century*, III (1812), 399.

[2] See below, p. xix.

[3] See above, p. xi, n. 1. That this work was used by the printer of *Essays and Criticisms* as copy for the ten essays in question is shown by two facts: first, that the texts in the two collections correspond in large part line for line; and second, that the dates given in *Essays and Criticisms* at the beginning of two letters taken from the *Bee* (III, 155, 159), while differing from the dates used by Goldsmith, agree exactly with those found in *The Beauties of the Magazines* (I, 229; II, 248).

turns out to be in the main a typical piece of
late eighteenth-century bookmaking, authorita-
tive possibly for the essays from the *Critical Review* and the *Westminster Magazine*, but otherwise of very dubious critical value.

It served as the basis, however, for the additions to Goldsmith's own selection of his essays
which were printed in the four-volume edition
of his *Miscellaneous Works* published in 1801 by
the combined booksellers of London. Into the
perplexing history of Bishop Percy's connection
with this edition there is no need to enter here,
for, apart from the fact that the whole story has
recently been told with admirable precision,[1] it
is unlikely that Percy had much to do with the
choice of texts to be included. From two letters written in the summer of 1798, to be sure,
it would appear that a copy of *Essays and Criticisms* had been sent him for his inspection,[2] and
the selection of unacknowledged essays given in
Volume IV may possibly, of course, have been
influenced by his response. But there is no evidence that such was the case, and in any event
the research involved in the selection certainly
did not go beyond the contents of *Essays and
Criticisms*, the publisher of which, it may be

[1] By Katharine C. Balderston in her *History & Sources of Percy's
Memoir of Goldsmith*, Cambridge, 1926.

[2] See *ibid.*, p. 45.

noted, was one of the booksellers responsible for
the new edition. Of the fifteen unacknowledged
essays printed in the fourth volume—three from
the *Westminster Magazine*, the rest from the
British—all had appeared in the 1798 collection;
the titles, supplied, for the most part, by the
earlier editor, were identical; the relative order,
a purely arbitrary one, was the same.[1] Why only
fifteen out of the thirty-seven new pieces in the
previous collection were retained is not clear; it
is difficult to believe, in view of the inclusion of
the "Belles-Lettres" series, that any genuine
criticism of authorship could have been involved, and it seems simpler on the whole to
assume that considerations of space and of the
supposed interest of readers were alone responsible for the decision.

A more serious regard for objective historical
fact was brought to bear on the problem a generation later when Prior published in 1837 his *Life
of Oliver Goldsmith* and his edition of the *Miscellaneous Works*. Whatever may have been Pri-
or's shortcomings as a biographer and an editor,
he clearly understood the importance of that
part of his task which obligated him "to discover
and to collect, as fully as possible, the scattered

[1] With one slight exception, too, all the notes and all the modifica-
tions in the text which are ascribed to Percy by Gibbs (see *Works*, I,
311, 316, 319, 389, 392) appear in *Essays and Criticisms*.

productions of his principal." The spirit in which he approached the problem may be seen from the following passage in his Preface to the *Life*:

Very little consideration made it apparent to the Editor, that Goldsmith must have written much which he had not thought proper to acknowledge; but to discover the nature of these labours, few of which from such a hand were likely to be worthless, he was thrown chiefly upon his own resources. . . . . The task of investigation proved toilsome and protracted. But a familiar acquaintance with his admitted writings, the habit of comparing them with pieces in periodical works to which he contributed, and with volumes issuing from booksellers by whom he was employed; coincidences of sentiment, repetitions of the same ideas or phraseology, in addition to general resemblance of style, afforded facilities for tracking him with considerable success.[1]

Prior's success in discovering hitherto-unknown contributions to periodicals, some of them certainly authentic, was indeed considerable. He was the first, for example, to determine by the help of Griffiths' marked copy, then in the possession of Heber, the extent of Goldsmith's labors for the *Monthly Review*.[2] He was the first to reveal Goldsmith's hand in the *Literary Magazine*.[3] He was the first to track him to the *Busy Body*.[4] He was the first to make known the serial publication in the *Lady's Magazine* of his

---

[1] *The Life of Oliver Goldsmith, M.B.* (London, 1837), I, xvii.

[2] *Ibid.*, pp. 225-31. [3] *Ibid.*, pp. 233-36. [4] *Ibid.*, pp. 334-36.

"Memoirs of M. de Voltaire."[1] And he was able, in addition, to establish as at least probable his authorship of several papers, not noted by earlier editors, in the *British Magazine*[2] and the *Public Ledger*.[3]

Valuable as was Prior's work, however, it was far from being definitive.[4] Although, unlike his predecessors, he usually took the trouble to state the grounds on which his new attributions rested, he was often satisfied with evidence of a loose and impressionistic sort; and although he read more widely than any earlier editor in the newspapers and magazines for which Goldsmith might have written, he by no means exhausted the possibilities of such sources, and his examination of the periodicals he did know was frequently casual and incomplete. Nor have his successors done much to fill the gaps he left. Cunningham, whose edition appeared in 1854,[5]

[1] *Life*, I, 304.

[2] *Ibid.*, pp. 344-52.   [3] *Ibid.*, pp. 353-64.

[4] The task of preparing the edition of Goldsmith's *Miscellaneous Works* which followed the *Life* later in 1837 seems to have been left by Prior to John Wright, a literary worker employed by the publisher, John Murray (see Peter Cunningham, *The Works of Oliver Goldsmith*, I, v; III, 138). This may explain why several of Prior's discoveries, including the essays in the *Literary Magazine*, did not appear in the edition and why, on the other hand, seven essays and eight reviews which had been included in the collection of 1798 were given as "now first collected." It may also explain the bad text of the "Memoirs of M. de Voltaire."

[5] *The Works of Oliver Goldsmith*, edited by Peter Cunningham, London, 1854. 4 vols.

had nothing to contribute except a more logical arrangement of the now traditional material and a passing hint of skepticism regarding the authenticity of the "Belles-Lettres" series.[1] Gibbs, who published in 1885 what is on the whole the most useful edition of Goldsmith,[2] included the essays in the *Literary Magazine* which had been identified but not reprinted by Prior,[3] and added two others on his own account from the same source;[4] but he broke no fresh ground. And since then, except for Miss Caroline Tupper's demonstration that Goldsmith could not have written the "Belles-Lettres" papers,[5] the canon of his periodical writings has been allowed to remain in the far-from-settled state in which it stood at the beginning of the present century.

To attempt to glean afresh in this field is not, therefore, quite so presumptuous an undertaking as might at first be thought. How far my efforts to do so have resulted in bringing to light genuine new writings of Goldsmith, it is of course for the reader to judge in the light of the detailed

[1] *Ibid.*, III, 260.

[2] *The Works of Oliver Goldsmith*, a new edition . . . . with notes from various sources, by J. W. M. Gibbs, London, 1885–86. 5 vols.

[3] *Ibid.*, IV, 417-28, 437-62.

[4] *Ibid.*, III, 450-57; IV, 429-36.

[5] *Publications of the Modern Language Association*, XXXIX (1924), 325-42. Miss Tupper's suggestion that the real author was Smollett is hardly more than a plausible guess.

evidence set forth in the notes. It may not be amiss, however, to point out briefly here the general nature of this evidence and, on the assumption that the great majority at least of the new essays will be accepted as authentic, to indicate what seems to me their value for the reader and student of Goldsmith.

II

It is impossible not to sympathize with the skepticism which has more and more of late been aroused by the attempts of critics relying solely or mainly on evidences of style and language to settle the authorship of anonymous literary works. The days of dogmatic attributions grounded merely on a general impression of manner or personality are happily long past. It is now universally recognized that we must follow the example of recent critics of painting and develop tests of authenticity which can be both stated and controlled objectively. But this, alas, is more easily said than done, and until we know a great deal more than we do now about the limits of individual variation in style and vocabulary, we must be content to employ such evidence, if at all, merely as a guide in research or as a check on conclusions reached by other methods. For this reason, though I feel satisfied that

all of the essays included in this collection are
in a style which Goldsmith could have written,
I have not based any positive argument upon
considerations of this sort. Fortunately, in the case of Goldsmith at any
rate, there is another type of internal evidence
which lends itself to somewhat safer use. More
than most writers of his distinction, Goldsmith
was under the necessity of husbanding his resources. His stock in trade of ideas, images, allusions was never large. Even in the domain
where his inventiveness was freest, that of comic
types and incidents, he achieved his effects with
a comparatively meager equipment of themes;
in those portions of his work—his early essays
and reviews, his two major poems, parts of *The
Vicar of Wakefield*—in which his concern was
chiefly with the exposition of ideas or the criticism of society, his inability or disinclination to
renew the contents of his own mind is more apparent still. Hence, no doubt, his plagiarisms;[1]

[1] See A. J. Barnouw, "Goldsmith's Indebtedness to Justus Van
Effen," *Modern Language Review*, VIII (1913), 314–23; R. S. Crane and
H. J. Smith, "A French Influence on Goldsmith's *Citizen of the World*,"
Modern Philology, XIX (1921), 83–92; R. S. Crane and J. H. Warner,
"Goldsmith and Voltaire's *Essai sur les mœurs*," *Modern Language Notes*,
XXXVIII (1923), 65–76; A. L. Sells, *Les sources françaises de Goldsmith*,
Paris, 1924; J. H. Pitman, *Goldsmith's "Animated Nature": A Study of
Goldsmith*, New Haven, 1924; H. J. Smith, *Oliver Goldsmith's "The
Citizen of the World*," New Haven, 1926; and J. E. Brown, "Goldsmith's
Indebtedness to Voltaire and Justus Van Effen," *Modern Philology*,
XXIII (1926), 273–84.

hence his habit, persisting from the *Bee* in 1759 to *An History of the Earth and Animated Nature* in 1774, of reprinting old work in new settings; hence, above all, his tendency to verbal and thematic repetition. How characteristic this last trait is must be evident to even the most casual student of his writings. Of the many examples that might be given from the works known certainly to be his, I select merely enough to afford a hint of the different forms which the habit assumed and to throw into proper relief the large element of verbal reminiscence which was a distinctive feature of the process.

Sometimes it is a simple phrase or image that is echoed, often with a slight difference of application, from work to work. Thus the beautiful lines at the beginning of *The Traveller*,

> Where'er I roam, whatever realms to see,
> My heart untravell'd fondly turns to thee;
> Still to my brother turns, with ceaseless pain,
> And drags at each remove a lengthening chain,[1]

are but a reincarnation in verse of the lament of Lien Chi Altangi in the *Citizen of the World*:

The farther I travel, I feel the pain of separation with stronger force; those ties that bind me to my native country and you, are still unbroken. By every remove, I only drag a greater length of chain.[2]

[1] Ll. 7-10.

[2] Letter III (*Public Ledger*, January 29, 1760).

So, too, the phrase which in the same poem sums up the present degradation of Holland,

> A land of tyrants, and a den of slaves,[1]

is identical with that which, four years earlier and likewise in the *Citizen of the World*, had been used to express the disgust of young Hingpo at the degeneracy of the modern Persians:

> Into what a state of misery are the modern Persians fallen! A nation famous for setting the world an example of freedom, is now become a land of tyrants, and a den of slaves.[2]

The frequent recurrence, in different contexts, of the simile of fermentation is a still more striking instance of the same thing.[3] Its earliest appearance is in *An Enquiry into the Present State of Polite Learning*:

> I forget whether the simile has been used before, but I would compare the man whose youth has been thus passed in the tranquillity of dispassionate prudence, to liquors which never ferment, and consequently, continue always muddy. Passions may raise a commotion in the youthful breast, but they disturb only to refine it.[4]

In 1761 it finds a place in the "Memoirs of M. de Voltaire":

> These youthful follies, like the fermentation of liquors often disturb the mind only in order to its future refine-

[1] L. 309.

[2] Letter XXXV (May 12, 1760). See below, p. 122, n. 1.

[3] On this figure see the note by Gibbs in *Works*, I, 407, and the comment of Caroline Tupper in *Publications of the Modern Language Association*, XXXIX (1924), 327–29.

[4] *Works* (ed. Gibbs), III, 501.

ment. A life spent in phlegmatic apathy, resembles those liquors which never ferment, and are consequently always muddy.[1]

It turns up, in 1764, in *An History of England in a Series of Letters:*

.... yet these struggles [the civil wars of the seventeenth century] at length ended in domestic happiness and security; the laws became more precise, and the subject more ready to obey, as if a previous fermentation in the constitution was necessary to its subsequent refinement.[2]

Finally, in a form somewhat closer to that of its original use, it is introduced into *The Life of Bolingbroke* (1770):

.... instead of aiming to excel in praiseworthy pursuits, Bolingbroke seemed more ambitious of being thought the greatest rake about town. This period might have been compared to that of fermentation in liquors, which grow muddy before they brighten; but it must also be confessed, that those liquors which never ferment are seldom clear.[3]

Sometimes the element repeated is a mere combination of proper nouns. Every reader of Goldsmith will remember the amusing use which he makes of the names Sanconiathon, Manetho, and Berosus first in the *Essays* (1765)[4] and then in *The Vicar of Wakefield* (1766).[5] Everyone will remember, too, the list of journalists' pseudonyms which appears, with but a slight change

[1] *Lady's Magazine,* II (1761), 293; *Works,* IV, 8. On the date of composition see *Works,* I, 450 and IV, 2.

[2] II, 43. Cf. *Notes and Queries,* CLIII (1927), 3–4.

[3] *Works,* IV, 183.

[4] *Ibid.,* I, 255. Cf. below, p. 107.   [5] *Works,* I, 125, 189.

of setting, in the same two works. In the *Essays* it is Goldsmith speaking (in the Preface) of the wholesale appropriation of his works by others:

If there be a pride in multiplied editions, I have seen some of my labours sixteen times reprinted, and claimed by different parents as their own. I have seen them flourished at the beginning with praise, and signed at the end with the names of Philantos, Philalethes, Philalutheros, and Philanthropos. These gentlemen have kindly stood sponsors to my productions, and, to flatter me more, have always taken my errors on themselves.[1]

In *The Vicar* it is George Primrose describing the ill success of his efforts to write for the magazines:

My little piece would therefore come forth in the midst of periodical publications, unnoticed and unknown. The public were more importantly employed than to observe the easy simplicity of my style, or the harmony of my periods. Sheet after sheet was thrown off to oblivion. My essays were buried among the essays upon liberty, eastern tales, and cures for the bite of a mad dog; while Philautos, Philalethes, Philelutheros, and Philanthropos, all wrote better, because they wrote faster than I.[2]

At other times the repetition is primarily of a theme or general idea, though even in such cases there is likely to be at least a slight verbal echo. Writing to Daniel Hodson on December 27, 1757, Goldsmith dwells on his homesickness for Ireland:

I confess I carry this spirit sometimes to the souring the pleasures I at present possess. If I go to the opera

[1] *Ibid.*, p. 245.   [2] *Ibid.*, pp. 158–59.

where Signora Columba pours out all the mazes of melody,
I sit and sigh for Lishoy fireside, and Johnny Armstrong's
Last Good Night, from Peggy Golden. . . . .

Before Charles came hither, my thoughts sometimes
found refuge from severer studies among my friends in
Ireland. I fancied strange revolutions at home; but I find
it was the rapidity of my own motion that gave an imaginary one to objects really at rest. No alterations there.[1]

This was too good to be forgotten, and we find
Goldsmith, in fact, utilizing the substance of
this passage on at least two later occasions. The
first is in the *Bee* for October 13, 1759:

When I reflect on the unambitious retirement in which
I passed the earlier part of my life in the country, I can-
not avoid feeling some pain in thinking that those happy
days are never to return. . . . . The music of Matei [the
Signora Columba of the letter] is dissonance to what I felt
when our old dairymaid sung me into tears with 'Johnny
Armstrong's Last Good Night,' or the cruelty of 'Barbara
Allan.'[2]

The second is in the *Citizen of the World* (August
13, 1760):

In every letter I expect accounts of some new revolutions in China. . . . . I open every packet with tremulous
expectation, and am agreeably disappointed when I find
my friends and my country continuing in felicity. I wan-
der, but they are at rest; they suffer few changes but what
pass in my own restless imagination: it is only the rapidity
of my own motion gives an imaginary swiftness to objects
which are in some measure immoveable.[3]

One more instance of this same type of repetition
may be given. In the *Public Ledger* for February

[1] *Works*, I, 431–32.   [2] *Ibid.*, II, 334.   [3] Letter LXIII.

18, 1760 (*Citizen of the World*, Letter XI), Goldsmith set forth a theory of the relation between happiness and luxury:

Am not I better pleased in enjoyment, than in the sullen satisfaction of thinking that I can live without enjoyment? The more various our artificial necessities, the wider is our circle of pleasure; for all pleasures consist in obviating necessities as they rise: luxury, therefore, as it increases our wants, increases our capacity for happiness.

Four years later he introduced the same theory, a propos of Switzerland, into *The Traveller:*

> Such are the charms to barren states assign'd;
> Their wants but few, their wishes all confin'd.
> Yet let them only share the praises due,
> If few their wants, their pleasures are but few;
> For every want that stimulates the breast,
> Becomes a source of pleasure when redrest.[1]

And he had not forgotten it when, toward 1770, he composed the chapter on "Sleep and Hunger" in *An History of the Earth and Animated Nature* (1774):

Every want thus becomes a means of pleasure, in the redressing; and the animal that has more desires, may be said to be capable of the greatest variety of happiness.[2]

Sometimes, finally, a whole passage is carried over from one work to another. There is a notable instance of this in two publications of the year 1759. In April, the following characterization of the Augustan Age in France and England

---

[1] Ll. 209–14.   [2] II (1774), 123–24.

appeared in *An Enquiry into the Present State of Polite Learning:*

But to blend these excellencies [those of Spain, Italy, and Holland], and arrive at perfection, seemed reserved for the poets and philosophers of England and France in the illustrious reigns of Queen Anne and Louis XIV. The writers of that period not only did honour to their respective countries, but even to human nature. Like stars lost in each other's brightness, though no single writer attracts our attention alone, yet their conjunction diffuses such brightness upon the age, as will give the minutest actions of those two reigns an importance which the revolutions of empire will want that were transacted in greater obscurity.[1]

In November, the same passage, modified slightly in details of expression, was made to apply to England alone in an essay in the *Bee:*

It was then [in the reign of Queen Anne] that taste was united to genius; and as before our writers charmed with their strength of thinking, so then they pleased with strength and grace united. In that period of British glory, though no writer attracts our attention singly, yet, like stars lost in each other's brightness, they have cast such a lustre upon the age in which they lived, that their minutest transactions will be attended to by posterity with a greater eagerness, than the most important occurrences of even empires which have been transacted in greater obscurity.[2]

A marked tendency to repetition growing out of a fundamental parsimony of idea and expression, accentuated no doubt by haste in composi-

[1] *Works*, III, 531.
[2] *Ibid.*, II, 444.

tion, is thus seen to be one of the distinguishing characteristics of Goldsmith's known writings.[1] This being the case, we ought to expect that between the productions which he himself signed and others which for one reason or another he did not see fit to acknowledge, there would be essentially similar coincidences of thought and phrase. That there are, in fact, numerous such coincidences between the papers reprinted in this volume and the works admitted to be his, a glance at my notes is sufficient to show. The correspondences are especially striking, I believe, in Essays II, III, IV, V, XIV, XVII, and XVIII. When, for example, we find the writer of "The Revolution in Low Life" saying of the former inhabitants of his deserted village that "though strangers to opulence, they were unacquainted with distress," and that they were "merry at Christmas and mournful in Lent, got drunk on St. George's-day, and religiously cracked nuts on Michaelmas-eve," and then recall that Goldsmith used almost the same words in *The Vicar* to describe the natives of the region to which the Primrose family migrated after their loss of fortune, we cannot but feel that we are witnessing exactly the same sort of literal

[1] Many more examples of the same tendency are pointed out by Gibbs in his notes to the *Works* and by Austin Dobson in his edition of the *Complete Poetical Works* (London, 1906).

transference of material as is exemplified by the foregoing quotations.[1]

It is obvious, of course, that evidence of this type must be used with great caution. There is always the possibility of borrowing, and we know only too well how prone Goldsmith was to pilfer from the writings of others.[2] There is always, too, the chance that what seems to be a repetition or anticipation by an author of himself is in reality to be explained as an independent reflection by two different authors of a common mode of thought or expression; and I am quite prepared to admit that certain of the parallels set forth in my notes may be accounted for in this way.[3] The supposition of a common background, however, loses much of its weight when the parallels, as is the case with many of those given here, involve passages of some length and of marked similarity or even identity in expression; and the hypothesis of borrowing, plausible enough when it is a question merely of a single similarity, surely becomes somewhat far fetched when, as, for example, in the four essays from the *Royal Magazine* (III–VI) or in "The Revolution in Low Life" (XVIII), the cor-

[1] See below, 116–17, and for other examples, pp. 14, 15–16, 26, 28, 38, 41, 43, 91–93, 95–96, 114, and 122.

[2] See the references given above, p. xxi, n. 1.

[3] This is particularly true, perhaps, of those given in the notes to Essays I and XIII.

respondences extend to several different known works of the supposed author, some of them earlier and some of them later in date of composition than the text in question.

But after all the case for Goldsmith's authorship of the papers here brought together does not rest entirely upon considerations of this sort. For all of them internal evidence may be supplemented by external, and that of two kinds. First, it can be shown from other sources that at or about the time the great majority of these papers were published Goldsmith was a more or less regular contributor to the periodicals in which they appeared. His connection with Smollett's *British Magazine* during 1760 has long been known; it is established by the fact that essays later acknowledged by him were printed in the issues for February, March, April, June, and October of that year.[1] That he was engaged in writing for Newbery's *Public Ledger* through the whole of 1760 and until at least the middle of August, 1761, is also a matter of common knowledge, and if contributions from his pen subsequent to that date have hitherto escaped notice, the explanation is merely, I suspect, that none of his editors has taken the trouble to examine a file of the paper after the conclusion of the

[1] See *Works* (ed. Gibbs), I, 275, 290; III, 428.

Chinese Letters on August 14; there is no reason
to suppose that his services ceased abruptly at
that time. His connection with Wilkie's *Lady's
Magazine* is likewise an old story; he was certainly a regular contributor from at least September,
1760, to the end of 1761;[1] and there is good
reason for accepting the statement of Percy, repeated by most subsequent biographers, that he
was the principal editor as well.[2] With regard

[1] Essay XXII of the collection of 1765 (on the rules drawn up by the
Empress Catharina for Russian assemblies) appeared in the September
number (II, 62–63); Essay XVII (on the character of modern English
preaching) was published in the number for December of the same year
(II, 195–99); and the "Memoirs of M. de Voltaire" ran in ten monthly
instalments from February to November, 1761. See the discussion of
other possible contributions in the Appendix, pp. 128–33, below.

[2] Percy says simply that "while he [Goldsmith] was writing his
Enquiry, &c. for Dodsley, he conducted for Wilkie the bookseller, a
Lady's Magazine . . . ." ("Life of Dr. Oliver Goldsmith," *Miscellaneous Works*, I [1801], 64). As Percy had been on familiar terms with
Goldsmith since early in 1759, it is hardly likely that he could have been
mistaken regarding the general fact which he thus records. His statement,
moreover, is confirmed by two other bits of evidence, which, taken in
combination, show that Goldsmith still held the position of editor in the
summer of 1761, shortly before the appearance of the two essays reprinted in this collection (XIII and XIV). The first is an entry in Percy's
MS "Memorandums extracted from Pocket Books relating to Dr. Goldsmith and the club at the Turk's Head in Gerrard Street" to the effect
that on May 25, 1761, he visited Goldsmith and turned over to him
material for a magazine which he was editing (summarized by Alice
C. C. Gaussen, *Percy: Prelate and Poet* [London, 1908], p. 142). The
second is the fact that a contribution by Percy actually appears in the
Lady's Magazine for June, 1761 (II, 487–89; published at the beginning
of July): it is the translation of the dialogue between Hervor and
Angantyr which he later included, with but very slight textual changes,
in his *Five Pieces of Runic Poetry* (London, 1763), pp. 13–20. How much
longer Goldsmith continued to hold the editorship is not certain—very
likely until the magazine was transferred from Wilkie to J. Cooke at the
beginning of 1762 (see III, 312). On the document used by Miss Gaussen, see Sir Ernest Clarke in *Proceedings of the Royal Society of Medicine*,
Vol. VII, Part II (1914), "Section of the History of Medicine," p. 94.

to the *Royal Magazine* and *Lloyd's Evening Post* the case is somewhat different, for no one, to my knowledge, has ever suggested any connection between Goldsmith and these two periodicals. It is possible, indeed, that the four essays here reprinted from the latter paper (XV–XVIII) were originally published elsewhere, perhaps in the *Public Ledger*, no complete file of which for the first half of 1762 seems to be known. On the other hand, should it be established that these essays were in reality written for *Lloyd's Evening Post*, that fact, though it cannot be used as a positive argument in support of Goldsmith's authorship, does not make against it; for among the principal shareholders of this paper was the man who more than anyone else at the time commanded his services, John Newbery.[1] The facts in the case of the *Royal Magazine* are much less ambiguous: not only was the publisher, J. Coote, associated with Newbery in various enterprises between 1760 and 1762,[2] but one of the best known of Goldsmith's acknowledged essays, the oriental allegory of "Asem, the Man-Hater," appeared in its pages in December, 1759.[3]

[1] See Charles Welsh, *A Bookseller of the Last Century* (London, 1885), pp. 161, 336.

[2] His name appears along with Newbery's on the title-pages of the *Lady's Museum*, of the *Christian's Magazine*, and of at least certain copies of the first edition of the *Citizen of the World* (see the advertisement of this last work in *Lloyd's Evening Post*, May 5–7, 1762).

[3] I, 296–99.

The second type of external evidence, valid
for nine of the eighteen essays, amounts to an
indirect acknowledgment by Goldsmith himself.
As is pointed out in the notes,[1] the six papers
taken from the *Public Ledger* (VII–XII) and the
three bearing the collective title "The Indigent
Philosopher" taken from *Lloyd's Evening Post*
(XV–XVII) form part of two series, the first
numbering in all eight essays, the second, four.
Now, of this total of twelve pieces Goldsmith
himself reprinted three as his own work—the
last of the second series as Essay IX in *Essays
by Mr. Goldsmith* (1765),[2] and the last two of the
first series as Essays XXVI and XXVII in the
second edition of the same collection (1766).[3] An
almost overwhelming presumption is thus established that he was likewise the author of the
remaining nine.

The case is not of course quite so complete
with respect to all the other essays included in
the volume. Concerning two of them, indeed, I
think there may well be some doubt. These two
—the first and the thirteenth—may perhaps be
ascribed to Goldsmith with as much assurance
as at least a dozen of the pieces added to the
canon by editors from Wright to Gibbs; but the

[1] See below, pp. 56, 98.

[2] See *Works*, I, 259–62.   [3] See *ibid.*, pp. 304–7, 307–10.

evidence hardly warrants more than a hypothesis, and I reprint them chiefly with a view to providing a starting-point for further investigation.[1] Sixteen others, however, remain, and concerning the genuineness of these it is difficult to see how there can be much question, so abundant and precise are the parallels with Goldsmith's acknowledged writings, so unequivocal the proofs of his connection with the papers in which they appeared.

III

To pretend that these sixteen essays (the authenticity of which I shall henceforth take for granted) represent Goldsmith at anything like his best would be to carry the enthusiasm of discovery to a ridiculous extreme. There is nothing here comparable to the most finished of the letters in the *Citizen of the World* or to such masterpieces among the *Essays* as "Asem" or the "Reverie at the Boar's-Head Tavern." If there are flashes of Goldsmith's characteristic humor in "The Indigent Philosopher" and at least a hint in "The Revolution in Low Life" of the social pathos that was to give warmth to *The Traveller* and *The Deserted Village*, it must be admitted that most of the new essays fall far be-

[1] A number of other doubtful essays, not printed here, are discussed in the Appendix.

low this level. The marks of the hard-pressed journalist are visible in all of them—in the thinness of much of the substance no less than in the negligence of the style. In an anthology of Goldsmith's most perfect pages none of them would find a place.

This is not to say, however, that they do not deserve to be reprinted. They are documents if no more, and as documents they supplement our existing knowledge of Goldsmith's work in a number of useful ways.

They help, for one thing, to enlarge our conception of the extent and variety of his journalistic activities between the end of 1759 and the middle of 1762. The familiar story of these years as told by all of his biographers includes mention of a few notices of books in the *Critical Review*, of the *Chinese Letters* and two or three other essays in the *Public Ledger*, of a dozen or more miscellaneous papers in the *British Magazine*, and of a somewhat vaguely determined rôle in the authorship and management of the *Lady's Magazine*. We now know that his services for the *Public Ledger* did not cease with the conclusion of the Chinese series; we are able to add a number of titles to the bibliography of his writings in the *British Magazine* and the *Lady's Magazine;* and we learn for the first time of his connection with the *Royal Magazine* and with *Lloyd's Evening Post*. These new facts are not, perhaps, very important in themselves, but in view of the obscurity which still envelops the early career of Goldsmith, they surely merit being placed on record.

More significant is the confirmation which these essays bring to a view of Goldsmith which recent scholarship has tended more and more to encourage. "Très au courant de la littérature et de la pensée françaises, il est un 'philosophe' à sa manière": this formula of M. Cazamian's[1] finds ample illustration in this volume. The essay on the effects of climate (II) and the four papers on the diversity of races and civilizations (III–VI) are especially interesting from this point of view. How largely they are indebted to Buffon for their details of anthropology and natural history may be learned from the notes. In a still wider sense—in their attempt at a panoramic view of society in the several regions of the globe, in their insistence on the potency of geographical and climatic conditions, in their recognition of the civilizing value of luxury, in their rejection of nationalistic bias—they reflect a current of ideas which was international in its

[1] E. Legouis and L. Cazamian, *Histoire de la littérature anglaise* (Paris, 1924), p. 873.

scope to be sure, but which, in 1760, undoubtedly had its most brilliant and influential repre-
sentatives in France. The papers on Avenbrugger's discovery of percussion (IX), on the efforts
of the Swiss to promote agriculture and other
arts (X), and on the debate over the size of men
(XI) are less important; but even they, superficial and journalistic as they are, afford useful
additional evidence of the interest which Goldsmith never ceased to feel in the scientific and
philosophical movements of the Continent.

Several of the new essays, again, shed fresh
light on the origin and meaning of a number of
Goldsmith's major works. The four articles in
the *Royal Magazine* provide a clue, hitherto lacking, to the interpretation of an interesting group
of papers in the *Citizen of the World:* such essays
as Letters X, XI, LXIII, LXXXII, LXXXVII,
XCI, and CVIII now become significant as frag-
ments in a larger scheme of sociological reflection, and in particular, it is possible to read the
defense of luxury in Letter XI without feeling,
as several commentators have done,[1] that it is
either an isolated or an insincere expression of
its author's thought. These same articles, moreover, together with two or three others in the

[1] See, for example, Gibbs's note in *Works*, III, 43, and Sells, *Les
sources françaises de Goldsmith*, pp. 120–21.

volume, permit us to enter more fully than was possible before into the genesis of Goldsmith's first important poem. *The Traveller* was not published until the end of 1764, but here in these essays of 1760–62, more completely than in any of the texts of this period previously known to us, we can witness the preliminary crystallization of the themes and attitudes of which it was to be composed. It is not merely that we can find here anticipations of this or that particular passage —the opening description of the homesick wanderer,[1] the picture of the childish sports of the modern Italians,[2] the portrait of the freedom-loving English:[3] such anticipations are to be met with elsewhere in the work of these years.[4] But nowhere else do we have such a clear foreshadowing as in Essays III and VI[5] of the general idea of a comparative survey of national psychologies which was to give unity to the poem; and nowhere better than in "Thoughts upon the Present Situation of Affairs" (XIV) and "The Revolution in Low Life" (XVIII) can we discover what lay back of the political and social pessimism which lent passion to its closing lines. "The Revolution in Low Life," it is hardly necessary to point out, is significant in still

[1] See below, pp. 12–14.   [2] P. 82.   [3] Pp. 52–55.
[4] See, for example, *Works*, II, 319; III, 17, 41, 190, 213, 342; V, 9, 52.
[5] See especially pp. 17–18, 50.

another connection. It is a first sketch of *The Deserted Village*—a sketch which antedates the finished poem by eight years and the short passage on rural depopulation in *The Traveller* by over two. No longer can we think of Goldsmith's concern with the woes of the countryside as a development merely of his later career; no longer can we fail to see how intimately the whole question was bound up in his mind with the speculations on trade and on national greatness and decline which had preoccupied him since the early part of the Seven Years' War. A new conception of the place and importance of *The Deserted Village* in Goldsmith's work is thus made possible, and incidentally we are given a precious bit of testimony in support of the view, even yet slightly heretical, that the immediate social background of that poem must be sought in England, not in Ireland,[1] and that, historically, the lament over the ruin of Auburn must be regarded as simply the most memorable of a long series of pamphlets called forth in the sixties and seventies of the eighteenth century by the English agricultural revolution.

Finally, if justification is still needed for the

[1] There is of course other evidence in favor of this interpretation. See, besides the familiar passages in *The Traveller* (ll. 393–412) and in the Dedication of *The Deserted Village*, the text from the *Public Advertiser* quoted below, p. 118, n. 1.

republication of these essays, it may perhaps be found in certain remarks of Goldsmith himself a propos of the *Miscellaneous Pieces* of Montesquieu. "There is a pleasure," he wrote, "arising from the perusal of the very bagatelles of men renowned for their knowledge and genius; and we receive with veneration those pieces after they are dead, which would lessen them in our esteem while living. . . . . Even a trifling poem of Swift or Pope will make a whole edition of their works sell with rapidity, and we now would purchase a warranted original copy of the worst verses Milton ever wrote, at ten times the price which the original copy of the 'Paradise Lost' brought him. We love to pursue genius from its serious occupations to its lighter and more airy amusements, and to peruse their unformed sentiments, as well as their finished pieces. Seeing their thoughts rise without order, connexion, or art, and destitute of the embellishments of style, and ornaments of learning, is examining them more closely, entering more intimately into their acquaintances, and more strongly marking their original powers."[1]

[1] *Works*, IV, 362–63.

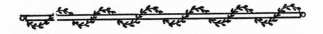

ESSAY I

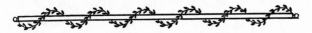

A LETTER SUPPOSED TO BE WRITTEN BY THE
MOORISH SECRETARY IN LONDON, TO
HIS CORRESPONDENT IN FEZ[1]

London, —— ——

IN MY last I gave you some account of our reception here; of the houses, philosophy, and strange customs of this proud people.[2] I shall confine my present letter only to their religion. The English profess their belief only in one Supreme Being, and pretend to pay their

[1] From the *British Magazine*, I (January, 1760), 31–32; reprinted in the *London Chronicle*, January 1–3, and in *Lloyd's Evening Post*, January 7–9. In spite of the general similarity in tone to *Citizen of the World*, Letter XLI (*Public Ledger*, May 28, 1760), and of the specific parallels noted below, I do not feel at all certain of Goldsmith's authorship of this essay. It is not even established that he had any connection with the *British Magazine* until February, 1760 (see above, p. xxxi), although one other essay in the January number—that on "The Bravery of the English Common Soldiers" (I, 37–39)—has been ascribed to him (see *Works*, III, 447–50, 457–59). On the other hand, if there is any basis for the tradition reported by Prior in 1837 (*Life of Oliver Goldsmith*, I, 360) that Goldsmith's first design for the series of essays which afterward became the *Citizen of the World* was "to make his hero a native of Morocco or Fez," it is not impossible that we have in this isolated letter, printed nearly a month before the first Chinese letter appeared in the *Public Ledger*, a surviving trace of the abandoned scheme. This possibility is my chief warrant for reprinting it here.

[2] In the "Memoirs of M. de Voltaire," written apparently in the early part of 1759 (see *Works*, I, 450), but not published until 1761,

I

adoration to him alone. But this is all a mere pretence; for, besides some living divinities, to whom they pay homage, there are a number of inanimate beings, to which every night they devoutly sacrifice:[1] and this you may be convinced I have from occular proof, in one of those *assemblies* where such rites* are performed, and where I casually happened to enter.

The first object that struck me was a large square altar, covered with green velvet, lighted by tapers in the middle, and surrounded by several persons, who are seated in the same manner as the Negroes, our neighbours, when they sacrifice to the moon.

* Lansquenet.

Goldsmith attributes to Voltaire the first clear realization that the ruling English characteristic is pride: "The French who before visited this island, were . . . . contented with . . . . transcribing a character of the people from former travellers, who were themselves unacquainted with our national peculiarities. Accordingly we find few of their books in which the English are not characterized as morose, melancholy, excessive lovers of pudding, and haters of mankind. . . . . Voltaire quickly perceived that pride seemed to be our characteristic quality; a source from whence we derived our excellencies as well as our defects" (*Lady's Magazine*, II, 480; *Works*, IV, 26). The pride of the English is also a recurring theme in Goldsmith's own writing in 1760 and later. See *Citizen of the World*, Letter IV (January 31, 1760): "The English seem as silent as the Japanese, yet vainer than the inhabitants of Siam. Upon my arrival I attributed that reserve to modesty, which, I now find, has its origin in pride"; also Letter V (February 7, 1760): ". . . . the pride of England"; and *The Traveller*, l. 327: "Pride in their port, defiance in their eye."

[1] Cf. *Citizen of the World*, Letter XLI (May 28, 1760): ". . . . were you not already acquainted with the religion of the English, you might, from my description, be inclined to believe them as grossly idolatrous as the disciples of Lao."

Upon my entering this assembly, one of the
members, who was apparently the sacrificing
priest, flung down on the altar several leaves of
a little book, which he held in his hand, one
leaf after the other. On each of these leaves were
represented several figures, very ill painted; but
which could be no other than the images of their
divinities: and of this I was soon convinced; for
as he distributed these pictures about, each of
the assistants laid on an offering, according to
the warmth of his devotion. I could easily observe, that these offerings were much greater
than those given up in their temples appointed
for universal worship.

After this part of the ceremony, the high
priest holds the rest of the little book in his hand,
which seems to tremble, and remains some time
as if struck with religious horror. All the assistants, attentive to what he is going to perform,
seem suspended and motionless also, like him.
Soon, however, he begins to turn the leaves,
while the assistants seem to suffer alternately
the most violent agitation, in proportion as the
spirit seems to have power over them.[1] One dis-

[1] Cf. the description of the behavior of the congregation at St. Paul's
in Citizen of the World, Letter XLI (May 28, 1760): "The idol which
they seem to address, strides like a colossus over the door of the inner
temple, which here, as with the Jews, is esteem'd the most sacred part of
the building. It's oracles are delivered in an hundred various tones; which
seem to inspire the worshippers with enthusiasm and awe: an old woman

plays his triumph with a roar of rapture; one fixes his eyes upon the image before him, and gnashes his teeth with rage and indignation: a third sits in gloomy silence, with all the passions by turns taking possession of his face. In short, they all seem so frightfully distorted, and suffer such changes of countenance, that they no longer appear to be human creatures. But no sooner has the high priest turned a certain leaf of the little book, than he himself becomes furious, tears the book, and sometimes eats it for vexation; overturns the altar, and curses the sacrifice. Nothing is heard but complaint, groans, and imprecations. Upon seeing them so transported, and so furious, I cannot forbear being of opinion, that the divinity they profess to adore is a jealous divinity, who, to punish them for sacrificing to another, gives them up each to a separate dæmon, to be tormented and disposed of at pleasure.

I am, &c.

who appeared to be the priestess, was employed in various attitudes, as she felt the inspiration. When it began to speak, all the people remained fix'd in silent attention, nodding assent, looking approbation, appearing highly edified by sounds, which to a stranger might seem inarticulate and unmeaning" (text of the *Public Ledger*).

ESSAY II

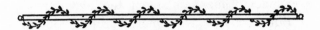

THE EFFECT WHICH CLIMATES HAVE UPON
MEN, AND OTHER ANIMALS[1]

To the Authors of the BRITISH MAGAZINE.

GENTLEMEN,

THE climate of Italy has, for several ages,
been different from what it was in the
times of the ancient Romans. Those sharp winters of which the ancients complained, are felt
there no longer: their rivers are now no where
seen frozen over, as in the times of Horace, the
fens of Ostia and Otranto being dried up: and
the appearance of volcanoes and mines of arsenic
serve to evince, that the country now is warmer
than it was about two thousand years ago. Need

---

[1] From the *British Magazine,* I (May, 1760), 127–29 [misnumbering
for pp. 311–13]; reprinted in *Lloyd's Evening Post,* June 9–11. The chief
reasons for ascribing this essay to Goldsmith are (1) that it was published
in a magazine to which he is known to have been at the time a regular
contributor (see above, p. xxxi); (2) that it reflects the same interest in
anthropological speculation and especially the same close dependence
upon Buffon as the four essays (III–VI in this collection) which began
to appear in the *Royal Magazine* a month later, and which are almost
certainly by him; and (3) that it treats a number of themes which he
afterward developed in his Introductions to R. Brookes's *New and Accurate System of Natural History* (1763) and in his *History of the Earth and
Animated Nature* (1774).

5

we then be at such a loss to account for the different manners of the ancient Romans and modern Italians? a warm country ever producing an effeminacy of manners among the inhabitants.[1]

But if Italy be grown more warm than it was some ages ago, we shall find other countries more cold. Iceland, and the northern parts of Siberia were temperate enough formerly to produce large trees in great abundance; as they are found to this day, if the inhabitants dig beneath the surface of the earth: at present they are hardly capable of producing the most stunted shrubs. From hence we see the reason why the ancient Scythians were so much superior to the modern Siberian Tartars. The Scythians, tho' they lived in the same country, probably enjoyed a milder climate, and were therefore brave, well-shaped, and enterprising: the modern Siberians, on the contrary, are dwarfish, cowardly, and insolent to the last degree: extreme cold producing the same inconveniencies with extremity of heat.[2]

[1] The same principle is implied in *An History of the Earth and Animated Nature*, II (1774), 225: "The warmth of the climate [in India] entirely influences their manners; they are slothful, submissive and luxurious: satisfied with sensual happiness alone, they find no pleasure in thinking; and contented with slavery, they are ready to obey any master."

[2] The same observation appears almost contemporaneously in the *Royal Magazine*, in the first of the series of four essays here ascribed to Goldsmith (see below, p. 19). It also occurs at least twice in *An History*

But countries themselves have not suffered such alterations as the inhabitants, who are transplanted from one climate to another. The Turks, who are the true descendants of the Scythians, properly so called, within these two centuries have not only begun to divest themselves of their ferocity, but have also departed from their original valour. They themselves scruple not to acknowledge this great difference between them and their ancestors: so that even a second time Greece has enervated its conquerors.

The Dutch colonists at Batavia seem to have quite forgot that parsimonious diet, and simplicity of manners, for which they have been remarkable in the other hemisphere, adopting all the luxurious manners of the Asiatics. After two or three generations at farthest, the blood loses its primitive qualities, and those of the climate manifest themselves in men, animals, and plants.

The Galatians, a colony of the hardy Gauls, lost all their original fierceness from a residence in the indulgent climates of Lesser Asia. The consul Memmius, seeing his soldiers terrified at

---

of the Earth and Animated Nature (see II [1774], 213, 236-37). It was probably suggested by Buffon. Cf. Histoire naturelle, III (1749), 527: "Mais lorsque le froid devient extrême, il produit quelques effets semblables à ceux de la chaleur excessive. ..."

the name of Gauls, encouraged them by justly observing, that the Galatians, softened by the luxuriancy of their country, no longer bore any resemblance to their intrepid ancestors.

Even the inhabitants of some of our own English colonies are said to suffer a change of character, consequent on this diversity of climate, and from being pensive, modest, and frugal, become vindictive, hasty, and profuse.

The effect of climates on the mind is by no means so striking as their apparent alterations on the body. The descendants of two Laplanders, who, with their wives, were brought into Denmark by the king's order,[1] meliorate in their stature and beauty in every generation; so that there are now some of their posterity, who, without mixing with the Danes, are however tolerably handsome.

The blackness which we find in the inhabitants between the tropics and elsewhere is merely the effect of climate.[2] Those Arabians who travelled from their native country, and planted themselves on the western coasts of Africa about three hundred years ago, are now grown, without any intermixture with the inhabitants, al-

[1] Cf. below, p. 20.

[2] Buffon had discussed this question and arrived at the same conclusion (op. cit., III [1749], 482–83).

most as black as the aborigines of the country.[1]
It may perhaps be asked, why the natives of
America, who live in the same latitude, are not
also black? but this doubt is obviated by the
first paragraph, which plainly proves, that countries, lying under the same latitude, may enjoy
a very different climate;[2] since there is shewn a
country, whose climate is different from that
which it was formerly known to have.

[1] Goldsmith refers to the same or a similar migration in *An History
of the Earth and Animated Nature*, II (1774), 228: "The Arabians themselves, many colonies of whom have migrated southward into the most
inland parts of Africa, seem to have degenerated from their ancestors;
and forgetting their ancient learning, with their beauty, have become a
race scarce any way distinguishable from the original natives." Cf.
Buffon's reference to the Ethiopians as "originaires d'Arabie" (*op. cit.*,
III [1749], 452).

[2] Goldsmith discusses this question at some length in his *History of
the Earth and Animated Nature*, II (1774), 233: "We could, therefore,
readily account for the blackness of different nations, did we not see the
Americans, who live under the line, as well as the Natives of Negroeland,
of a red colour, and but a very small shade darker than the natives of the
northern latitudes, in the same continent. For this reason, some have
sought for other causes of blackness than the climate; and have endeavoured to prove that the blacks are a race of people, bred from one man,
who was marked with accidental blackness. This, however, is but mere
ungrounded conjecture; and, although the Americans are not so dark as
the Negroes, yet we must still continue in the ancient opinion, that the
deepness of the colour proceeds from the excessive heat of the climate.
For, if we compare the heats of Africa with those of America, we shall
find they bear no proportion to each other. . . . ." The source of the
arguments in both passages was doubtless Buffon (see *op. cit.*, III [1749],
484, 514). Taken by itself, therefore, the parallel proves only that the
writer of this essay in 1760 and Goldsmith in 1774 had been reading the
same book and had been impressed by the same passage in that book.
But the coincidence becomes more striking and consequently more difficult to explain except by an assumption of identical authorship, if we
consider that the writer of the essay belonged, as did Goldsmith at the
same time, to the relatively small circle of contributors to the *British
Magazine*, and that when it was written Goldsmith himself was almost
certainly engaged in reading Buffon. See the notes to the next three essays.

Let us then be contented in accounting for
the variety of the human species, to attribute
it to the diversity of climate alone.[1] It is this
which may truly be said to place the distinction
between the tall German and the inhabitant of
Greenland but four feet high.[2] It is climate alone
which tinctures the negroes skin; that makes the
Italians effeminate, and the Briton brave.

Even other animals change their nature as
well as men.[3] On the coast of Guinea, where dogs
are carried in considerable numbers, as they
serve for food to the barbarous natives, the
spaniel and the grey-hound, the lap-dog and the
mastiff, after a few descents, lose every distinction, and become an animal with pricked ears,

---

[1] Cf. Buffon, *op. cit.*, III (1749), 519–20. In *An History of the Earth
and Animated Nature,* Goldsmith allows for the operation of other causes
as well. Cf. II (1774), 239: "In this slight survey, therefore, I think we
may see that all the variations in the human figure, as far as they differ
from our own, are produced either by the rigour of the climate, the bad
quality, or the scantiness of the provisions, or by the savage customs of
the country."

[2] Cf. below, p. 19: "This whole race of men [the inhabitants of the
polar regions] are generally but four feet high, the tallest not above four
feet and an half. . . . ."

[3] Cf. Goldsmith's Introduction to Vol. I of Brookes's *New and Accurate System of Natural History* (1763): "We have observed, that among
animals of the same kind there is little variety, except what is produced
by the art of man; but we would have this observation extend only to
animals of the same climate. As in the human species many alterations
arise from the heat or cold, and other peculiarities of the region they
inhabit, so among brute animals the climate marks them with its influence, and in a few successions they entirely conform to the nature of their
situation" (*Works,* V, 85).

and a rough skin, somewhat resembling a wolf.[1]
Let us wisely respect those dispensations of nature, which thus adapts the inhabitant to the
soil, and makes the rudest climates most agreeable to its proper natives.[2]

[1] There is a somewhat vague reference to this same phenomenon in
the text from which I have quoted in the preceding note (*Works*, V, 85–
86). Cf. also *An History of the Earth and Animated Nature*, II (1774), 329:
". . . . those dogs which with us have long hair, when carried to Guinea,
or Angola, in a short time cast their thick covering, and assume a lighter
dress, and one more adapted to the warmth of the country."

[2] Cf. *An History of the Earth and Animated Nature*, II (1774), 217:
"The wretched natives of these climates seem fitted by Nature to endure
the rigours of their situation." A still closer parallel occurs in the first
of H.D.'s articles in the *Royal Magazine*, in the passage beginning, "There
cannot be a stronger instance of Providence having naturally fitted us
to the climate than this . . . ." (see below, pp. 21–22).

ESSAY III

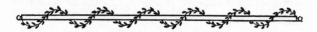

A COMPARATIVE VIEW OF RACES AND NATIONS[1]

To the Author of the ROYAL MAGAZINE.

SIR,

O Felices Nimium, bona si sua Norint Anglicani![2]

THE traveller, who after an absence of fifteen years revisits his native country, feels a joy which it is impossible to express. That spot which gave him birth, how rude, how barbarous soever, has beauties beyond the most charming

---

[1] From the *Royal Magazine*, II (June, 1760), 285–88. The June number was published on July 1 (see the advertisement in the *Public Ledger* for that date).

Goldsmith's authorship of the series of four essays of which this is the first would seem to be established beyond reasonable doubt by the parallels assembled in the notes. Coincidence is excluded by the precision, extending in many cases to verbal echoes, of the correspondences; and though borrowing might be invoked to explain certain individual parallels, it can scarcely be made to explain them all in view of the fact that the acknowledged writings of Goldsmith from which they are taken are some of them earlier and some of them later in date than the essays in question.

For Goldsmith's earlier connection with the *Royal Magazine*, see above, p. xxxiii. The first three of the four essays are starred as being "originals" in the newspaper advertisements of the issues in which they appeared (see, for example, the *Public Ledger*, July 1, 26, and August 1, 1760); stars are not used at all in the advertisements of the issue containing the fourth essay (*ibid.*, October 1, 1760).

The essays bear no titles in the *Royal Magazine*.

[2] Adapted from Virgil *Georgics* ii. 458–59.

scene that ever art improved or fancy painted.
Placed on his native mountain, the returning
wanderer feels an happiness beyond whatever
the vales of Caprea, or the orange-groves of
Naples, could afford; finds more solid satisfaction in cultivating his little kitchen-garden at
home, than when indolently stretched beneath
the luxuriant shades of Pisa.

The Scotchman who wish'd for an estate in
Arno's vale, that he might sell it and buy one
at home in the highlands, was not so ignorant
as we at first might be apt to imagine: those
dear relatives he had left behind, might have
enhanced the value of his country.[1] To grow old
in the same fields where we once were young; to be
capable of every moment beholding objects that
recal [sic] our early pleasures; to measure our
own years by the trees that our hands have planted, are more truly pleasing than may at first be
imagined. We entertain for every mountain,
stream, or cottage, that we have been accustomed
to see, an habitual fondness; and each is capable
of improving our sensations. "Methinks," says
the sensible Menage, "I would not wish to see

[1] There is a similar story in Goldsmith's letter to Daniel Hodson,
December 27, 1757 (*Works*, I, 431): "Surely my affection [for Ireland]
is equally ridiculous with the Scotchman's, who refused to be cured of
the itch, because it made him unco' thoughtful of his wife and bonny
Inverary."

even an old post removed with which I had been long acquainted."[1]

After a life of the most dissipated variety, after having strayed through so many countries without being regarded, or known, with what enthusiasm do I again revisit the happy island where I drew my first breath, and received the early pleasures and institutions of life? After so many fatigues, dangers, discontents; after seeing so many millions of faces, without finding one friend among the number,[2] to be again restored to my country, my friends, my relations, to a competency for life; what rapture, what poignant satisfaction? here let me spend the small remainder of my days in tranquillity and content: here let the rest of my life be passed in attempts to improve my fellow-creatures: let the last running of that current be useful, which has hitherto been exhausted in a vain search for

[1] Goldsmith used the same quotation in a similar context in the *Public Ledger* for September 12, 1760 (*Citizen of the World*, Letter LXXIII): "Our attachment to every object around us encreases in general, from the length of our acquaintance with it. I would not chuse, says a *French* philosopher, to see an old post pulled up, with which I had been long acquainted" (text of the *Public Ledger*).

[2] Cf. the "Letter from a Traveller" in the *Bee*, No. I, October 6, 1759 (*Works*, II, 319): "When will my wanderings be at an end? When will my restless disposition give me leave to enjoy the present hour? . . . . It is now seven years since I saw the face of a single creature who cared a farthing whether I was dead or alive." Cf. also *The Traveller*, ll. 1–10, 23–30.

something new,[1] in restless and unsatisfying curiosity![2]

Hail Britain, happiest of countries! happy in thy climate, fertility, situation, and commerce; but still happier in the peculiar nature of thy laws and government. Examine every state in Europe, and you will find the people either enjoying a precarious freedom under monarchical government, or what is worse, actually slaves in a republic, to laws of their own contriving. What constitutes the peculiar happiness of Britain, is, that laws may be overlooked without endangering the state. In a mere republic, which pretends to equal freedom, every infringement upon law is a dissolution of government, and must consequently be punished with the most unremitting severity; but in England, laws may be sometimes overlooked without danger.[3] A King who has it

[1] Cf. the title of chap. xx of *The Vicar of Wakefield:* "The history of a philosophic vagabond pursuing novelty, but losing content."

[2] The sentiment in this and the preceding paragraph is somewhat similar to that expressed in *The Deserted Village*, ll. 83–96.

[3] Less than a fortnight before this essay appeared Goldsmith had discussed this same theme at greater length but in remarkably similar language in the *Public Ledger*, June 19, 1760 (*Citizen of the World*, Letter L): "How then are the English more free (for more free they certainly are) than the people of any other country whatever? The prerogative which they enjoy above all other Democratic governments *is, that the severity of their laws may be relaxed without endangering the constitution.*

"In all those governments, where laws derive their sanction from the *people alone*, transgressions cannot be overlooked without bringing the constitution into danger. In every republic the laws must be strong,

in his power to pardon, gives the government
at once the strength of the oak, and the flexibility of the yew.[1]

England is not less happy with respect to
climate: the almost continual spring of Italy,
does not indeed adorn our fields; but if we want
their spring, we are also without their sultry
summer. We have no occasion to pant after the
valleys of Hæmus, or wish for the deep embow-
ering shade: our summers are less warm, and
our winters are to the senses less cold, than those
of any other country.

These are some of the many advantages we
enjoy above the rest of mankind; nature pours
her gifts round us, and we only want a proper
temper to enjoy them. I should esteem it my

---

because the constitution is feeble. . . . . Thus in Holland, Switzerland,
and Genoa, as I am told, new laws are not frequently enacted, but the
old ones are observed with unremitting severity.

"In a monarchical state, in which the constitution is strongest, the
laws on the contrary may be relaxed without danger; for though the
people should be unanimous in the breach of any one in particular, yet
still there is an effective power capable of enforcing obedience, whenever
it should be proper to observe the law either towards the support or
welfare of the community.

"In republics therefore the people are slaves to laws of their own
making, and in unmix'd monarchies they are slaves to the will of one who
is subject to frailties like themselves. In England, from a variety of happy
accidents, their constitution is just strong enough to permit a relaxation
of the severity of laws, and yet those laws still remain sufficiently strong
to govern the people" (text of the *Public Ledger*).

[1] Goldsmith had used the same metaphor in the essay quoted in the
preceding note: "The constitution of England, is at present possessed
of the strength of its native oak and its laws of the flexibility of the
bending tamarisk.

greatest happiness, could my travels conduce to
form such a temper; could they make one individual more happy in himself, or more useful to
society; could I enlarge one mind, and make the
man who now boasts his patriotism, a citizen of
the world; could I level those distinctions which
separate mankind; could I teach the English to
allow strangers to have their excellencies;[1] could I
mend that country in which I reside, by improvements from those which I have left behind.

"In whatever part of the world fortune
pleases to throw me, whatever character she
gives me to act," says the Tyanean of old,[2] "let
me consider mankind as my friends, and think
myself at home. The brown Indian and the
pallid Gaul, in my eyes, only differ in external
covering: the polished Athenian and the savage
Thracian have their peculiar virtues, and what
one attains by refinement, the other makes up
by sincerity. Where-ever I turn, I find the earth
peopled with many fools, some villains, and but
few that are wise."

In all the circle of knowledge, there is not

[1] A brief statement of a theme which Goldsmith was to develop more
fully in the *British Magazine*, August, 1760. See *Works*, I, 320–23. The
phrase, "a citizen of the world," had already occurred several times in
his writing. See *ibid.*, III, 74, 86, 531; IV, 41.

[2] Cf. *Citizen of the World*, Letter VII (February 4, 1760): "From
Zerdusht down to him of Tyanea, I honour all those great names who
endeavour to unite the world by their travels. . . . ."

perhaps a more pleasing employment, than that
of comparing countries with each other; if the
traveller happens to be possessed of talents
equal to the enquiry; who knows where to dilate,
and where to be concise; who with a well-direct-
ed understanding passes hastily through the
howling wilderness or sandy desart, but enjoys
the cultivated spot, the peopled valley, with an
abiding delectation.

Come then, and let us take a view of this
earth in which providence has placed us; let us
at least examine the out-lines of the universal
plan; let us survey the various customs of the
inhabitants. To compare the individuals of one
nation with each other, has been performed by
others: to consider nations in the same light as
individuals, and to improve our native customs
by whatever appears praise-worthy among foreigners,[1] has been hitherto unattempted; it
makes a subject at once replete with instruction
and entertainment.

Beginning northward,[2] we shall find that

[1] This is a favorite theme in Goldsmith. See his review of Van
Egmont's *Travels* in the *Critical Review*, June, 1759 (*Works*, IV, 361) and
especially *Citizen of the World*, Letter CVIII (February 27, 1761), later
reprinted as Essay XVIII in *Essays by Mr. Goldsmith* (1765).

[2] The details that follow on the polar races are for the most part
taken from Vol. III (1749) of Buffon's *Histoire naturelle*, in the chapter
entitled "Variétés dans l'espèce humaine." Most of them were later introduced by Goldsmith into his *History of the Earth and Animated Nature*
(1774), sometimes in a phrasing that is closer to that of the present essay
than to the original of Buffon.

those regions bordering on the artic circle, or
approaching the pole, bear a strong similitude
to each other; we there behold a race or species
of men of a small stature, and dwarfish figure;
the immoderate cold of those regions, has almost
the same effect upon the body as an excess of
heat; their colour almost approaches blackness,
and their faces are as savage as their manners.
This whole race of men are generally but four
feet high, the tallest not above four feet and an
half; they have a large head, with lank black
hair, a large flat nose, a yellowish deep brown
eye, eye-brows turning upwards at their temples,
their cheek-bones extremely high, their lips hideously thick, and their mouths wide in proportion; a squeaking voice, a lean habit, and
strength which is amazing to the beholder.[1]

[1] Cf. Buffon, *op. cit.*, III (1749), 371–72: "En parcourant dans cette
vûe la surface de la terre, & en commençant par le nord, on trouve en \
Lapponie & sur les côtes septentrionales de la Tartarie une race d'hommes
de petite stature, d'une figure bizarre, dont la physionomie est aussi
sauvage que les mœurs. ... Tous ces peuples ont le visage large & plat,
le nez camus & écrasé, l'iris de l'œil jaune-brun & tirant sur le noir, les
paupières retirées vers les temples, les joues extrêmement élevées, la
bouche très-grande, le bas du visage étroit, les lèvres grosses & relevées,
la voix grêle, la tête grosse, les cheveux noirs & lisses, la peau basanée; ils
sont très-petits, trapus quoique maigres; la pluspart n'ont que quatre
pieds de hauteur, & les plus grands n'en ont que quatre & demi." The
corresponding passage in *An History of the Earth and Animated Nature*
is in one or two respects somewhat closer to our text. See II (1774), 213–
14: "The first distinct race of men is found round the polar regions. . . . .
These nations being under a rigorous climate, where the productions of
Nature are but few, and the provisions coarse and unwholesome, their
bodies have shrunk to the nature of their food; and their complexions
have suffered, from cold, almost a similar change to what heat is known
to produce; their colour being a deep brown, in some places inclining to

Heaven seems to adapt the inhabitants to the miserable region in which they are placed: nature is there frozen up in almost endless winter, all the vegetable productions are stunted in their growth, and nothing appears to an European eye but endless horror and desolation. Yet these poor people, happy in their native stupidity, are perfectly satisfied, enjoy the uncertain meal with a voracious pleasure, and desire no more; for they know no better.

Even the highest delicacies of Europe have no relish with them: the King of Denmark, willing to civilize this people, ordered two of the inhabitants to be brought from their native mountains to Copenhagen; yet all the flattery, and all the amusements of the Danish court had no effect upon them; they languished for some time after their native country, one of them ventured out to sea in a little boat, and was never heard of more, and the other soon after died of grief for the absence of his companion.

actual blackness. These, therefore, in general, are found to be a race of short stature, and odd shape, with countenances as savage as their manners are barbarous. The visage, in these countries, is large and broad, the nose flat and short, the eyes of a yellowish brown, inclining to blackness, the eye-lids drawn towards the temples, the cheek-bones extremely high, the mouth very large, the lips thick, and turned outwards, the voice thin and squeaking, the head large, the hair black and straight, the colour of the skin of a dark greyish. They are short in stature, the generality not being above four feet high, and the tallest not above five."

There cannot be a stronger instance of Providence having naturally fitted us to the climate than this. How different these from the indolent Spaniard, or voluptuous Persian:[1] they seem almost of a different species, and some men do not more differ from brutes than those from each other. Strangers to jealousy or shai..c, they bathe altogether, men and women, and are not in the least afraid of being seen naked. Nay, they offer to strangers the use of their wives and daughters, and think themselves highly honoured when their offer is accepted.[2] Their cloathing is of skins of deer, of wild fowl, or seals, having no such thing as linen among them:[3] their food is of dried fish, and the flesh of deer and bears; their bread fish-bones bruised to a powder, and mixed with the tender bark of pine or birch-trees; their drink whale oil and water, with an

[1] In the *Public Ledger*, May 12, 1760 (*Citizen of the World*, Letter XXXV), Goldsmith had contrasted the slavery of the modern Persian, condemned to minister to the luxury of the great, with the freedom of the "houseless Tartar of Kamschatka."

[2] Cf. Buffon, *op. cit.*, III (1749), 376: "Ils se baignent nuds & tous ensemble, filles & garçons, mère & fils, frères & sœurs, & ne craignent point qu'on les voie dans cet état. ... Ils offrent aux étrangers leurs femmes & leurs filles, & tiennent à grand honneur qu'on veuille bien coucher avec elles ..." ; and *An History of the Earth and Animated Nature*, II (1774), 216: "With regard to their morals, they have all the virtues of simplicity, and all the vices of ignorance. They offer their wives and daughters to strangers; and seem to think it a particular honour if their offer be accepted."

[3] A close translation of a sentence in Buffon, *op. cit.*, III (1749), 376.

infusion of juniper-berries;[1] their habitations are dug almost entirely under ground, and always filled with smoke; in winter to keep them warm, and in summer to keep away the gnats, with which their country abounds, notwithstanding the severity of the season.[2]

This is a picture of nature, conforming to the hard rules of necessity. Knowledge would only serve to make them miserable, only shew them the horrors of their situation, without lending them a clue to escape. They seem made for the climate they inhabit; a climate which they love, and they only can love. Here, amidst rocks, in winter covered with snow, and in summer with moss, they lead a life of contented solitude,[3] each couple living by themselves, and seeking a separate sustenance. While we surround the globe, in order to satisfy our fictitious wants, these savages are contented with an happy indolence; nor do they desire to be informed whether the earth has any other inhabitants besides themselves.

---

[1] Cf. *An History of the Earth and Animated Nature*, II (1774), 216: "Their food is principally dried fish, the flesh of rein-deer and bears. Their bread is composed of the bones of fishes, pounded and mixed with the inside tender bark of the pine-tree. Their drink is train-oil, or brandy, and, when deprived of these, water, in which juniper berries have been infused." Both passages are close translations of Buffon, *op. cit.*, III (1749), 375.

[2] A paraphrase of Buffon, *op. cit.*, III (1749), 376–77.

[3] Cf. the similar description of the contentment of the Swiss in *The Traveller*, especially ll. 199–210.

Here then are whole nations who live without laws, and are destitute of all ideas of social intercourse, except that between the sexes. Neither motives of fear, nor of universal benevolence, have induced them to cultivate society. Man in a state of nature never seeks society, or desires the sanction of law, if he has nothing to lose;[1] it is property only that draws men into communities, and may be properly said to form a people.

Your's, &c.

H. D.[2]

[1] Goldsmith applied this principle to the native of Siberia in the *Public Ledger*, October 10, 1760 (*Citizen of the World*, Letter LXXXII): "In like manner his happiness will incline him to bind himself by no law: Laws are made in order to secure present property, but he is possessed of no property which he is afraid to lose. . . . ."

[2] I have no explanation to offer for these initials. A fondness for impersonation, however, was characteristic of Goldsmith at this time; witness the two travel essays in the *Bee* (*Works*, II, 319–21 and 329–33) and the contemporary *Chinese Letters* in the *Public Ledger*.

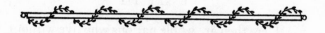

ESSAY IV

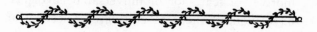

The Same Subject Continued[1]

To the Author of the Royal Magazine.

SIR,

AS YOU thought proper to give my letter a place in your last (See p. 285.) I shall, without any farther apology, pursue the subject of comparing nations with each other: a subject pregnant both with entertainment and utility.

If we compare those hideous regions that lie within the arctic circle, with the very opposite part of the globe, those countries which approach the southern pole, we shall find human nature in the latter inhabiting even still more deplorable circumstances. The natives of New Holland, either in figure or understanding, are scarcely raised above the brutes,[2] while the brutes there seems [*sic*] to enjoy an astonishing

---

[1] From the *Royal Magazine*, Supplement to. Vol. II, pp. 340–43. According to an advertisement in the *Public Ledger*, this number was published on July 26, 1760.

[2] Cf. Buffon, *Histoire naturelle*, III (1749), 408: "Les habitans de la côte de la nouvelle Hollande ... sont peut-être les gens du monde les plus misérables, & ceux de tous les humains qui approchent le plus des brutes. ..."

share of sagacity. It is well worthy of remark, that in every country, in proportion as the natives seem stupid and barbarous, the other animals are sagacious and cunning. Thus the ape, the beaver, the elephant, bred in the inland parts of Africa, seem almost as wise as the inhabitants themselves; but particularly in this country, there are some creatures like rats, of an amphibious nature, which testify a degree of docility, far surpassing what we commonly observe in the brute creation. They seem to understand the duties of society, have their little polities, and even surpass the ignorant inhabitants, who are vainly privileged with reason, in their well-observed institutions.

From the solitary lives the natives lead in this country, it must not be expected they can make any progress in knowledge: it is to society alone that man owes his superiority, and those who either from accident, or from the nature of the country in which they are born, have been deprived of this advantage, scarce seem possessed of the intellects even of a monkey. In proportion as men cultivate society, they become more sagacious; and all the other little communities among animals, which subsisted during human solitude and ignorance, when men come, to unite against them, are dissolved: the beaver is no longer an architect, nor the elephant a citizen; as men become more social, their knowledge and understanding seems to forsake them, and in proportion as these become more polite, those degenerate into stupidity.[1]

Thus we see each extreme of our globe inhabited by rude barbarians, and what is still a more melancholy truth, by beings, who, from the nature of the climate and country, are incapable of being reduced into society, or any

[1] This observation recurs frequently in Goldsmith. "Naturalists assure us," he had written in *An Enquiry into the Present State of Polite Learning* (1759), "that all animals are sagacious, in proportion as they are removed from the tyranny of others. In native liberty, the elephant is a citizen, and the beaver an architect; but whenever the tyrant man intrudes upon their community, their spirit is broken, they seem anxious only for safety, and their intellects suffer an equal diminution with their prosperity" (*Works*, III, 469-70). Cf. also the *Bee*, No. IV, October 27, 1759 (*Works*, II, 369-70): "Animals, in general, are sagacious, in proportion as they cultivate society. The elephant and the beaver show the greatest signs of this when united; but when man intrudes into their communities, they lose all their spirit of industry, and testify but a very small share of that sagacity, for which, when in a social state, they are so remarkable." After 1760 the idea is found in his Introduction to Vol. I of Brookes's *New and Accurate System of Natural History* (see *Works*, V, 78, 85), and at least twice in his *History of the Earth and Animated Nature*. Cf. II (1774), 328: "In those countries where men have seldom intruded, some animals have been found, established in a kind of civil state of society. Remote from the tyranny of man, they seem to have a spirit of mutual benevolence, and mutual friendship. The beavers, in these distant solitudes, are known to build like architects, and rule like citizens. . . . . But as soon as man intrudes upon their society, they seem impressed with the terrors of their inferior situation, their spirit of society ceases, the bond is dissolved, and every animal looks for safety in solitude, and there tries all its little industry to shift only for itself"; and IV, 157: "In all countries, as man is civilized and improved, the lower ranks of animals are repressed and degraded. . . . . Their feeble arts quickly disappear, and nothing remains but their solitary instincts. . . . ." The source of this last passage, as Goldsmith's note acknowledges, is Buffon (*op. cit.*, VIII [1760], 282-83).

degree of politeness. The only motives that can induce men to enter into society, are either the fears of a combination from other animals, an incapacity of subsisting upon ones own labour, or a country too small for the number and manner of living of the inhabitants, and consequently a dread of each other. But those people have not one of these motives to induce them to be social; the animals are neither in sufficient number, or furnished with a proper degree of strength in those cold climates, to be formidable, and consequently to produce a combination against them upon the motives of self-defence. Their labours, which consist in hunting or fishing, supplies [*sic*] a sufficient, though precarious subsistence, and are best carried on singly, a society of hunters and fishers being inconvenient for many reasons. And as for the country, it is sufficiently extensive and incapable of culture, so that the inhabitants must of consequence be few: they must be fishers or hunters, they must have no motives to invade the property of others, and have no property of their own to lose.[1]

[1] Goldsmith gave essentially the same explanation of why the inhabitants of the northern wilds do not become social in the *Public Ledger*, October 10, 1760 (*Citizen of the World*, Letter LXXXII). Cf. above, p. 23, n. 1.

They are denied the refinements of sense, and it is impossible therefore to introduce philosophy among them. Though sensual refinement has ever been the great object of philosophic scorn, though declamation has set its face against luxury, and speculation deprecates bodily pleasure; yet luxury ever preceded wisdom, or, in other words, every country must be luxurious before it can make any progress in human knowledge. Sensuality first finds out the pleasure, and wisdom comments on the discovery.[1]

The Indians of America, for example, when the members of the academy of Sciences at Paris went over to Quito, in order to measure a degree near the equator, were surprized at the folly and inutility of so long a journey. They said they set no value on such knowledge, nor could they see

---

[1] This paragraph bears a striking resemblance to two passages in Goldsmith's *Citizen of the World*, the one published earlier than the present essay, the other later. The first is in Letter XI (*Public Ledger*, February 18, 1760): "I confess it sounds fine in the mouth of a declaimer when he talks of subduing our appetites, of teaching every sense to be content with a bare sufficiency, and of supplying only the wants of nature; but is there not more satisfaction in indulging those appetites, if we can do it with innocence and safety, than in restraining them? . . . . Examine the history of any country remarkable for opulence and wisdom, you will find they would never have been wise had they not been first luxurious; you will find poets, philosophers, and even patriots, marching in luxury's train. The reason is obvious; we then only are curious after knowledge when we find it connected with private [so the *Public Ledger* text, which I am quoting here; the edition of 1762 has "sensual"] happiness. Sense ever points out the way, and reflection comments upon the discovery." The second passage is in Letter LXXXII (October 10, 1760): "A desire of enjoyment first interests our passions in the pursuit [of knowledge], points out the object of investigation, and reason then comments on the discovery" (text of the *Public Ledger*).

either profit or amusement in the acquisition. It would be unnatural if they did; for as it was no way connected with their ideas of happiness, and consequently but little suited to their curiosity, they found as little pleasure in knowing it, as a polite European would in an exact admeasurement of Saturn's ring. But had luxury first introduced the silks or the commodities of China among them, and had they been assured that by an exact knowledge of the globe, navigation would be improved, and silks imported cheaper, to know then the measure of a degree at the equator, would be instructive and entertaining.[1]

From hence we may conclude, that the inhabitants of either pole, as their country is incapable of affording the luxuries of life, are consequently in a state of helpless and hopeless ignorance, without knowledge at present, and incapable of receiving any for the future.

[1] Cf. *Citizen of the World*, Letter XI (February 18, 1760): "Inform a native of the desert of Kobe, of the exact measure of a degree upon the equator, he finds no satisfaction at all in the information; he wonders how any could take such pains and lay out such treasures in order to solve so useless a difficulty, but connect it with his happiness, by shewing that it improves navigation, that by such an investigation he may have a warmer coat, a better gun, or a finer knife, and he is instantly in raptures at so great an improvement" (*Public Ledger* text). The expedition of the Académie des Sciences to South America is also alluded to in Letter LXXXII (October 10, 1760): "The barbarous Siberian is too wise, therefore to exhaust his time in quest of knowledge, which neither curiosity prompts, nor pleasure impels him to pursue. When told of the exact admeasurement of a degree upon the equator at Quito, he feels no pleasure in the account. . . . ."

Before we leave these countries, it may be re-
marked once for all, that as regions in opposite
parallels of latitude, bear in general a striking
similitude to each other with regard to vegetable
productions and the face of the landscape, but
widely differs [*sic*] with regard to the human
inhabitants; the nations which lie within the
southern hemisphere are universally more barbarous, the country less cultivated, and the inhabitants more thinly scattered. Here then are
regions, even more beautiful, than those northern ones which we inhabit, still desolate. To
what can we ascribe this seeming vacancy in
nature? To an obvious cause; man first began
to exist in the northern hemisphere, and his
descendants have not since crossed the line in
sufficient numbers, they nor their posterity, to
people those extensive wilds; and as these countries are not populous, so consequently they are
unpolite. This serves at once to refute the opinion of the human race, being propagated from
several sources in different parts of the globe,
and shews the manifest absurdity of those who
have lately revived the ancient doctrine of man's
being indigenous, or sprung from the soil; because then the most beautiful kingdoms would
be best stocked with inhabitants, which is contrary to known observation.

Leaving those inhospitable climates, if we
travel from Greenland southward beyond the
arctic circle, we shall find the almost immeasur-
able dominions of Russia, which extending from
Finland to Kamkatska, occupy the greatest part
of the northern hemisphere; there seems no
counterpoise to this on the opposite hemisphere,
unless we suppose some countries lying round
the south pole, more extensive than have been
hitherto discovered.

It is natural for every government to mark
their dominions as extensively as possible, when
they are sure of their pretensions being never
called in question; for this reason the Russians
lay claim to several countries they know scarcely
by name, and pretend a right to wilds, when they
have none but the tygers of the forest to oppose
their claims. It is true they have built forts
along some of the navigable rivers, and Cossack
soldiers are scattered up and down at immense
distance from each other; but they may be truly
said to be masters of this country, because there
are none found to dispute their pretensions.

Though this extensive dominion lies under
such a variety of climates, yet all its provinces
may be said to resemble each other in this, that
the inhabitants are equally ignorant, I had almost said barbarous; though perhaps what we

may call barbarous will be found to be a state most consentaneous to our nature. They universally live in society; observe in general the duties of morality towards each other with the strictest sincerity: travellers universally speak of the honesty of almost all the Tartar nations subject to the Russian empire, even to strangers. Their houses are but mean, yet still they have no idea of better; their food is coarse but wholsome, and must be acquired by exercise.

Perhaps this is the true point of happiness, on one side of which lies savage wretchedness, and on the other excruciating refinement.[1] A life like this, of society, frugality, and labour, is the object of every philosophic wish, the theme of every enraptured imagination. The manner in which the Tartars now live, is the same with that of all unpolished nations, while the inhabitants had room enough, while they had no enemy to fear, except the hungry lion or insidious tyger; but it differs widely from their manner of living, who have entered into large associations, not through fear of brute animals, but of each other; who make war, not upon the inhabitants of the forest, but men.

[1] Cf. Goldsmith's *History of England in a Series of Letters*, I (1764), 30: "There is a period, between natural rudeness and excessive refinement, which seems peculiarly adapted for conquest and war, and fits mankind for every virtuous and great atchievement"; and the text quoted in the next note.

While this simple happy people have room
enough to spread (and that they will probably
have for some centuries more) they will make
but a slow progress towards refinement; they
must first become populous, and then they will
be no longer ignorant. When that period ar-
rives, provided they still continue united under
one head, Europe may tremble for her liberties;
she will probably behold new myriads of com-
batants pouring down from the North, as she
once saw them marching from the borders of
the Caspian sea.[1]

But let us not imagine those nations entirely
happy; they have their enemies as well as we:
of all forests upon earth, theirs are most infested
with wild beasts, which often issue in formidable
numbers and wage open war. The bear, the hy-
ena, the wolf, and the lynx, here dispute the
dominion with man, who vainly arrogates the
title of being Lord of the creation. Neither art
or courage often avail any thing against their
numbers and fierceness; and sometimes all the

[1] Cf. *Citizen of the World*, Letter LXXXVII (*Public Ledger*, October
31, 1760): "Believe me, my friend, I can't sufficiently contemn the
politics of Europe, who thus make this powerful people arbitrators in
their quarrel. The Russians are now at that period between refinement
and barbarity, which seems most adapted to military atchievement, and
if once they happen to get footing in the western parts of Europe, it is
not the feeble efforts of the sons of effeminacy and dissention, that can
serve to remove them. The fertile valley and soft climate will ever be
sufficient inducements to draw whole myriads from their native desarts,
the trackless wild, or snowy mountain" (text of the *Public Ledger*).

inhabitants of several villages have been known to be devoured.

Whence arises the necessity of those noxious animals? Would it not have been better, if Providence had furnished the globe with harmless creatures, adapted only to feed upon the fruits of the earth, fit emblems of celestial innocence? Providence is in this very instance particularly wise. The earth was made in order to support the greatest number of animals possible: it is most consistent with the goodness of an all-wise Creator, to give being to as many creatures as his earth would nourish. Were all animals therefore to live upon the fruits and herbs of the field, they could not possibly subsist in such numbers as they now do, as there would not be a sufficient quantity of food to supply them. But as some live upon the fruits, and are food for others, which in turn are themselves a prey to the most rapacious of all, thus every chasm in nature is filled, and no vacant space left in the page of universal beauty.

Though the manners of all the Tartars are in general the same, yet nothing has so much surprised travellers, as the difference there is to be found in their persons, and that subsisting in countries not very remote from each other. The Kalmucks, for instance, are described as hideously ugly, thick lipped, flat nosed, tawny complexioned, broad, squat, and ill-proportioned; the inhabitants of the neighbouring Circassia are finely shaped, fair, with large eyes, and regular features.[1]

Instead of attempting to account for so strange a phænomenon myself, I shall only repeat the sentiments of a late ingenious French writer on the subject. He takes in the first place some pains to prove, that the Chinese are originally a colony of the ancient Egyptians, who were either sent there as travellers, merchants, or conquerors. This he proves from the similitude of their manners, their methods of communicating their ideas by writing, their pyramids, and some other striking similitudes.[2] The Circassians he takes to have been a colony left on the way; and

[1] This contrast between the Kalmucks and the Circassians was perhaps suggested by Buffon (see *op. cit.*, III [1749], 381, 384). There are frequent references to these two peoples in Goldsmith's work in 1760 and 1761 (see *Works*, III, 18, 155, 196, 222, 224, 413).

[2] Goldsmith was familiar with this theory, for he ridiculed it in the *Public Ledger*, November 21, 1760 (*Citizen of the World*, Letter LXXXIX) in a passage translated from Voltaire's *Histoire de l'Empire de Russie sous Pierre le Grand*, I (1759), xvi–xvii (see *Modern Philology*, XXIII [1926], 277–78). I have not been able to identify the "late ingenious French writer" with any certainty. He was probably not Joseph de Guignes, whose *Memoire dans lequel on prouve, que les Chinois sont une colonie Egyptienne* (Paris, 1759) is concerned merely with the argument from writing. It is possible that the reference is to Dortous de Mairan, whose *Lettres ... au R. P. Parrenin, ... contenant diverses questions sur la Chine*, likewise published in 1759, makes use of all three of the arguments mentioned in this sentence (see especially pp. 47–51, 87–88, 214–18), though it contains nothing that could have suggested the remark in the next sentence about the Circassians.

this he endeavours to prove from the resemblance in person to those two nations already mentioned, and their being unlike many of the neighbour nations around them.

I am, &c.

H. D.

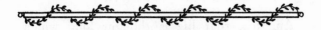

ESSAY V

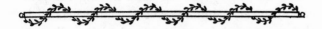

THE SAME SUBJECT CONTINUED[1]

To the Author of the ROYAL MAGAZINE.

SIR,

IN MY last I considered the inhabitants of the Tartarian countries, their manner of living, and the happiness that attended it. I shall pursue the interesting subject, and remark the differences and resemblances that subsist between the natives of a barbarous and a polite nation.

The first difference, in comparing a barbarous with a polite nation, that visibly offers, is the longevity of the inhabitants of polished countries, above the savage tenants of the forest. A life of seventy, eighty, and even an hundred years, is very common in several parts of Europe, where the inhabitants are reduced into fixed society; but through all the wilds of Tartary, nay, if we extend the view to the northern parts

---

[1] From the *Royal Magazine*, III (July, 1760), 3–6. This issue appeared on August 1 (see the advertisement in the *Public Ledger* for that date).

of America, that life is thought long which reaches three-score.

The vicissitudes of season, the long fastings, the consequent repletion upon finding the precarious meal, swimming rivers, while warm with the chase, and long protracted vigils, all contribute to shorten the human span, and no habitude can reconcile them to our natures. From hence we see how very wrong those parents are, who attempt to improve the health and strength of their children by too hardy an education; and though some may survive such attempts, they seem insensible how many die under the experiment. Peter the Great, in order to teach some children to be perfect sailors, instituted, that they should be permitted to drink only sea-water; their instructors obeyed the order, but all the children died.[1]

There are still however some physical causes which contribute to keep the inhabitants of those extensive regions barbarous; and among the rest may be reckoned the want of corn. In

[1] Cf. Goldsmith's essay on education, first printed in the *Bee*, No. VI, November 10, 1759, and later republished, with some changes, in the *Essays* of 1765 (see *Works*, II, 404): "We know, that among savages, and even among our peasants, there are found children born with such constitutions, that they cross rivers by swimming, endure cold, thirst, hunger, and want of sleep, to a surprizing degree; that when they happen to fall sick, they are cured without the help of medicine, by nature alone. Such examples are adduced to persuade us to imitate their manner of education, and accustom ourselves betimes to support the same fatigues. But had these gentlemen considered first, that those savages and peasants

those countries, which lie even in a more southern latitude than England, the inhabitants find
that they are incapable of producing corn. To
what shall we attribute this surprising defect?
Not to the soil, for that is at once deep and fertile, nor to the coldness of the climate, for colder
climates in Europe produce corn in abundance:
to their immense forests alone can this defect
of vegetation be ascribed. Every tree has its
own humid atmosphere around it, insomuch
that farmers generally find their neighbourhood
noxious to fields of corn; a forest of trees, by
loading the atmosphere with too much humidity, is still more hurtful. If we examine the soil
upon which forests stand, we shall in general find
it cold, moist, and covered with water; in such
therefore it cannot be expected corn should be
produced in any quantities; and even tho' the
forests should be cleared away, yet this cannot
be done to such a sufficient extent as to prevent
the humidity of the wide-extended neighbouring

---

are generally not so long lived as they who have led a more indolent life:
Secondly, that the more laborious the life is, the less populous is the country. Had they considered, that what physicians call the *stamina vitae*, by
fatigue and labour, become rigid, and thus anticipate old age. That the
number who survive those rude trials, bears no proportion to those who
die in the experiment. Had these things been properly considered, they
would not have thus extolled an education begun in fatigue and hard-
ships. Peter the Great, willing to enure the children of his seamen to a life
of hardship, ordered that they should only drink sea water, but they
unfortunately all died under the experiment" (text of the *Bee*).

forest, to injure every labour of the husbandman.

Thus we see every country capable only of
a gradual improvement, as well with regard to
its natural qualities, as to the moral character
of its inhabitants. The soil must first be cleared,
not in spots, but in tracts, the most extensive,
before it acquires any degree of fertility; the inhabitants must become numerous before they
grow polite.[1]

Attempting to introduce polite manners into
a barbarous and ill-peopled country, is as vain
an endeavour, as by clearing a way in the midst
of a forest, to attempt to produce corn. Politeness may be introduced into any country too
soon; and in that under our notice this actually
has been the case.

Their great monarch Peter erroneously fancied, that by sending the inhabitants of a polished country, to people those desolate regions,
he would improve the original inhabitants in the
duties of society; time however has shewn, that
those unhappy gentlemen who were banished to
this region of desolate sterility, were incapable
of introducing happiness among the natives;

[1] Cf. *Citizen of the World*, Letter LXXXII (October 10, 1760): "No,
my friend, in order to make the sciences useful in any country, it must
first become populous. . . . ." The principle is stated by Buffon, *Histoire
naturelle*, III (1749), 489–90.

with all their arts and knowledge, were even more helpless than the meanest of the natives. Nature, that true benefactor of mankind, quickly evinced, that savage customs were the most fit for savage inhabitants. The polite Europeans, with all those refined desires of education, and liable to all those wants which arise from close connected society, found themselves among a people, whose only wish was to live, who placed more happiness in the greatness than delicacy of the meal, who were unaccustomed to these fictitious wants, which arise when our real necessities are supplied; who were insensible how those, who wanted no sensual enjoyment, could still be unhappy: what then could missionaries do in such a country? They were, instead of refining the inhabitants, obliged to comply with their barbarous manners; and instead of bringing over the country from barbarism, they became themselves barbarians.[1]

Peter should have behaved as the Portuguese

[1] The same illustration is found in *Citizen of the World*, Letter LXXXII (October 10, 1760): "No, my friend, to attempt to introduce the sciences into a nation of wandering barbarians is only to render them more miserable than even nature designed they should be. A life of ignorance is best fitted to a state of solitude. The great lawgiver of Russia thus attempted to improve the desolate inhabitants of Siberia, by sending among them some of the politest men of Europe. But the consequence has shewn, that the country was as yet unfit to receive them; they languished for a time with a sort of exotic malady, and at last, instead of rendering the country polite, they conformed to the soil, and put on barbarity" (text of the *Public Ledger*).

did, in similar circumstances, to the polite
Chinese, already instructed in the luxuries of
life. They sent missionaries, who were capable
of improving them in speculative knowledge,
and the sciences, and such messengers were glad-
ly received: to the wild Americans, they, on the
contrary, sent men who had less learning and
more perseverance, men who were capable of
instructing the inhabitants how to cultivate the
earth, and to improve the productions of nature.

Let us then here pause, to consider the wisdom of man in suiting himself to the climate, the
soil, the society in which he has been born.
Those peculiarities, which we are too apt to call
barbarous, because they differ from our own, are
often the effect of fine contrivance and well-
guided sagacity. Should we, for instance, condemn the clumsy shoe of an inhabitant of the
north, how justly might he laugh at our ignorance, since they prevent him from sinking in the
deep snows, with which the country is generally
covered? Should we call the Tartar barbarous,
because he eats his horse, would he not justly
deride our delicacy, since the flesh of animals,
as they approach the north, is in general more
tender than that of southern animals; and horse-
flesh in Tartary is probably the greatest delicacy
they have? Should we object to his fondness for

distilled milk, who knows but this may be a delicacy yet untasted in Europe, as the preparation is certainly a chymical secret unknown to the politest European, who are [sic] incapable of extracting a spirit from milk?[1] Should we condemn them for keeping the bodies of the dead much longer than we; they may justly answer, that with them bodies are found not to corrupt so soon as with us; and as no inconvenience attends this custom, it is but an innocent mark of respect to the dead. If their language be defective and barren, they have but few ideas, and consequently do not want a language more copious. They want an exalted understanding; and happy it is for them that they labour under this defect. The greatest understanding of an individual, doomed to procure food and cloathing for himself, can but barely supply him with expedients to prolong his existence from day to day. But should we suppose him one of a large community, performing only his share of the common business, he then gains leisure for intellectual pleasures, and enjoys the happiness of reason and reflection.

[1] Cf. the *Public Ledger*, February 27, 1761 (*Citizen of the World*, Letter CVIII): "There is scarce any country how rude or incultivated soever, where the inhabitants are not possessed of some peculiar secrets, either in nature or art, which might be transplanted with success; thus, for instance, in Siberian Tartary, the natives extract a strong spirit from milk, which is a secret probably unknown to the chymists of Europe" (*Public Ledger* text).

Proceeding in our intellectual map, we now descend lower, to those happy climates possessed by the polite inhabitants of the temperate zone, where the soil has been fertilized by long culture, where the river glides in a channel not its own, where all nature seems to put on the face of art, where the brute animals are in perfect subjection, and calmly receive laws from man; to regions, along which the surveyor has laid his measuring-line, where every lawn and fountain is claimed by some proprietor.

Happy were it for those climes, did not the same inconveniencies arise from too great a population, which in the countries already described proceed from being too thinly inhabited. The more a country is peopled to a certain degree, the better; but there is a point beyond which even a multiplicity of inhabitants render each other unhappy. It is then that penal laws are encreased, that wars are engaged in, which in the end only serve to lessen the number. Among polite nations, whatever may be the pretext for war, if it be examined to the bottom, it will be found to proceed from a nation, by long peace becoming too numerous, and consequently desirous of occupying those regions possessed by another: instigated by the same motives, the rival nation answers the challenge, both fight;

some two or three hundred thousands are slain
on either side; and each nation thus diminished
of its inhabitants, now begins to look round, and
to find that the survivors are not too numerous
to destroy each other's internal welfare. Thus a
peace is concluded, which leaves both nations in
the very same circumstances in which they began the war; with this only difference, that the
inhabitants on both sides are reduced, and more
nearly proportioned to the extent of the country
which they possess.

If we compare the encrease of a colony newly
planted, with that of an equal number of the
mother-country at home, we shall in general
find, that the former breed up five children for
one bred up by the latter. In the mother-country, from being already too populous, marriages
are not entered into, as the contracting parties
are not able to maintain their offspring: in
colonies, where a proper extent of country is
presupposed, nothing more than increase of
labour is sufficient to maintain a numerous
progeny, which growing up, are soon able without further assistance to maintain themselves.
Thus colonies have ever cultivated commerce
rather than war, until they could spread no
farther; and then, from the natural inconvenience of too great population they arrived at,

attempting to invade that property among their neighbours by force, which they were unable to possess by legal means. War, therefore, unceasing war, is the consequence of refined society: it is a natural evil, which arises from the nature of an happy society. The inhabitants of every well regulated society must increase; and every country is capable of supporting only a determinate number of inhabitants.

If we compare the bodies of the inhabitants of the temperate climates with those which lie to the north or south, we shall find the pores of the skin much larger than in any other part of the globe, and a manifest difference in this particular. Excessive heat or cold contract the pores of the skin; and those who have been long accustomed to either, are found no way subject to those profuse sweats, which in every part of Europe are the consequences of labour: from hence the Europeans derive a longer continuance of youth and vigour; for their bodies daily losing on one part, and receiving new supplies on another, are continually changing; and, if I may so express it, are thus always new: whereas in the cold and hot climates, the bodies of the natives do not receive so easily addition and loss, and consequently continue more constantly the same. This will sufficiently account for the difference between climates, in respect to youth and age; an inhabitant of the north, or the equator, is old at twenty-five, but continues to support nature in this state of premature debility for several years; while an European, on the contrary, seldom feels either the effects, or discovers the wrinkles of age, till he is past fifty, and then declines into the vale of years with precipitation.

That permanent vigour of the body is also the most proper to supply a fund of materials to supply the mind; as the soul often sympathizes with the decaying outward frame, before an inhabitant of the frigid or torid zone has an opportunity of growing learned, he is grown old: the season for memory and invention is past; and he is, from the natural infirmities consequent upon age, more desirous of preferring the acquisitions of knowledge he has made, than of treasuring up new. On the contrary, the philosopher of the temperate climate, has a long period in which to collect his inductions; and as from the nature of the climate, a greater variety of objects offer instruction, so he has a longer period to enjoy the fruits of his acquisition.

Your's, &c.

H. D.

ESSAY VI

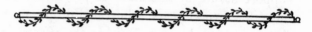

THE SAME SUBJECT CONTINUED[1]

To the Author of the ROYAL MAGAZINE.

SIR,

IF WE compare the inhabitants of Europe with those of the other parts of the globe, the latter will appear not much superior to the fabled satyrs of antiquity, and possessed of little more of humanity than the appearance. It is true, the Turks, Persians, and Indians, have their schools for learning as well as we: in Constantinople, Grand Cairo, Ispahan, and Agra, there are professors appointed by the state to instruct the nobility in astronomy, geometry, arithmetic, poetry, and the Arabic language; but their learning, instead of opening the mind, only adds obstinacy and vanity to their ignorance: so that they labour under all the errors of falsehood, and all the pride of pedantry.

[1] From the *Royal Magazine*, III (September, 1760), 138–40 (published on October 1); reprinted in the Limerick *Magazine of Magazines*, XX (September, 1760), 236–38, and in the *Imperial Magazine*, I (October, 1760), 525–27. Though the essay is unsigned, it is evident from the first and fifth paragraphs that it belongs to the series which began in the June number.

It is a subject worthy consideration, how it comes to pass that those countries which enjoy so much fertility, and so happy a climate, where the inhabitants have not only leisure to cultivate philosophy,.but have frequent admonitions to that purpose, in many of the books of their law: it is a matter of surprise, I say, how these countries, which were the first to nurse infant science, and to divulge it to the world; who, after a long succession of ignorance, once more under the Arabian caliphs emerged into politeness; it is surprising how they have relapsed into more than the pristine barbarity.[1]

The kingdoms of Asia Minor are by no means so populous now as formerly, and that from the defects of its government; while one part of the country is too closely inhabited, another part is seen without any inhabitants at all; a country becomes steril by too much or too little cultivation, hence the whole face of nature is changed at length, here into spots worn out by too fre-

[1] Both the substance and the rhetoric of this paragraph are closely paralleled in a passage which Goldsmith had published in the *Public Ledger*, August 13, 1760 (*Citizen of the World*, Letter LXIII): "Yet believe me, my friend, that even China itself is degenerating from her antient greatness; her laws are now more venal, and her merchants more deceitful than formerly; the very arts and sciences have run to decay. .... Whence this degeneracy in a state so little subject to external revolutions, how happens it that China, which is now more powerful than ever, which is less subject to foreign invasions, and even assisted in some discoveries by her connexions with Europe; whence comes it, I say, that the empire is thus declining fast into barbarity!" (*Public Ledger* text.)

quent tillage, there into tracts grown wild and barren from want of human culture. As every country becomes barren, it is proportionably depopulated; and as the people diminish, so do the love, and even the utility of the sciences diminish also.[1]

Hence we see how the inhabitants of Asia are more savage than those of Europe; where the whole domain is divided into small districts, and governed with equity; where the inhabitants are more equably diffused, and where all find in mutual distrust mutual security.

The difference between the Asiatics and Europeans is striking and obvious; and even the natives of the east themselves acknowledge our mental superiority. But it is a more difficult task, and requires a more acute discernment, to be able well to describe the minute differences which obtain among the respective countries of Europe, compared with each other; to ascertain the genius and character of each, how far it proceeds from accident, climate, government, or religion; and to represent the whole uninfluenced by resentment, and unbiassed by national partiality.[2]

To begin with Ireland, the most western part

[1] Cf. above, pp. 30, 33, 40.

[2] In the *Public Ledger*, February 4, 1760 (*Citizen of the World*, Letter VII), Goldsmith had defined the task of the philosophic traveler in similar terms: "Let European travellers cross seas and deserts merely

of the continent, the natives are particularly remarkable for the gaiety and levity of their dispositions: the English, transplanted there, in
time lose their melancholy serious air, and become gay and thoughtless, more fond of pleasure, and less addicted to reasoning. This difference of disposition cannot properly be said to
arise from climate or soil, which is in general the
same as in England; but merely from the nature
of their government. They live in a fruitful
country, sequestered from the rest of mankind,
protected by a powerful nation from foreign
insult; and regardless of neighbouring greatness,
they have no important national concerns to
make them anxious, or cloud their tempers with
the solemnity of pride. In such circumstances
they are contented with indolence and pleasure,
take every happiness as it presents, are easily
excited to resent, and as easily induced to sub-
mission.

Scotland, till of late, had in itself the power

---

in order to measure the height of a mountain . . . . , but what advantage
can accrue to a philosopher from such accounts, who is desirous of understanding the human heart, who seeks to know the *men* of each country,
who desires to discover those differences which result from climate, religion, education, prejudice, and custom. . . . . How many travellers are
there who confine their relations to such minute and useless particulars?
For one who enters into the genius of those nations with whom he has
conversed . . . . there are twenty who only mention some idle particulars,
which can be of no real use to a true philosopher" (text of the *Public
Ledger*). The source of this earlier passage was d'Argens' *Lettres chinoises*
(see *Modern Philology*, XIX [1921], 86–87).

as well of foreign as domestic administration; a consciousness of power, and a long continued government, always produces a love of one's country. The Scotch therefore are still partial to their country-men,[1] and jealous of their country's honour. The cause of these passions first implanted among them, has ceased with the discontinuance of national administration; but the effects are still visible, and may continue so for several ages. Their country is barren, and consequently the people are frugal; it would be absurd for the natives to indulge the same desire for pleasure, that those of the country before-mentioned entertain; for this would be to create wants which it is not in the power of nature to satisfy. Their frugality brings several other virtues in its train; they have fortitude in adversity, because they have from their youth been taught to suffer; and they have moderation in prosperity, for it is seldom that those who have been bred frugally during the younger part of life, after a certain age gain new tastes for luxury and refinement.

The English are not less divided from the rest of the world by the circumfluent seas, than differing from them in their manners, disposi-

[1] Cf. *Citizen of the World*, Letter V (February 7, 1760): ". . . . the pride of England, the absurdity of Ireland, and the national partiality of Scotland. . . . ."

tions, and turn of thinking: and these peculiarities may be ascribed partly to the government, and partly to the climate and soil.[1] As the government is charged with the most important concerns of Europe, and as every man has some share in the government, he by this means acquires a conscious importance, and this superinduces that gloom of solid felicity which foreigners have mistaken in some for melancholy and spleen: the soil is fruitful, and this prompts to luxury; but as those necessaries which are eaten are produced in greater plenty and delicacy than those which are drank, in other words, as the soil produces the most excellent meats, but no wine, the inhabitants are more apt to indulge an excess of eating than drinking; and this has a mechanical effect upon the tempers: it encreases their seeming severity, so that they are grave without phlegm, and apparently ill natured with hearts sympathising with every distress. They are distinguished from the rest of Europe by their superior accuracy in reasoning, and are in general called the nation of philosophers by their neighbours of the continent;[2]

[1] Cf. the title of *Citizen of the World*, Letter XCI (as given in the collected edition of 1762): "The influence of climate and soil upon the tempers and dispositions of the English."

[2] The superiority of the English in reasoning is the theme of *Citizen of the World*, Letter CXXI (not in the *Public Ledger*): "Whenever I attempt to characterize the English in general, some unforeseen difficulties

this superiority of reason is only the consequence of their freedom;[1] they pursue truth wherever it may lead, regardless of the result; and unawed by power, give a loose to the most hidden workings of the mind: wherever philosophy takes root in a country of freedom and solemnity, it must certainly flourish; the one gives courage to pursue the literary adventure, and the other gives perseverance in the journey.

It has long however been a doubt, whether the passion for liberty, now implanted among the English, be merely the result of accident; or whether it proceeds from the influence of external causes, or whether an Englishman is naturally more fond of freedom than others, who are unacquainted with the happiness of its effects.

If we regard some other animals which the

---

constantly occur to disconcert my design; I hesitate between censure and praise. When I consider them as a reasoning, philosophical people, they have my applause; but when I reverse the medal, and observe their inconstancy and irresolution, I can scarcely persuade myself that I am observing the same people.

"Yet, upon examination, this very inconstancy, so remarkable here, flows from no other source than their love of reasoning. . . . .

". . . . The people of Asia are directed by precedent, which never alters; the English, by reason, which is ever changing its appearance."

Cf. also the description of the English in *The Traveller*, especially ll. 325-26:

> "Stern o'er each bosom reason holds her state,
> With daring aims irregularly great."

[1] Cf. *The Traveller*, ll. 335-36:

> "Thine, Freedom, thine the blessings pictur'd here,
> Thine are those charms that dazzle and endear."

country produces, and consider their impetuosity, their fierceness, their courage, and how they lose those qualities when they leave the soil, we shall be apt to attribute that impatience of servitude, which the English are so very remarkable for, to physical causes.[1]

They have ever been noted for a jealousy of their privileges, and even in the times of the Romans were remarkable for treating strangers with severity, whom they fancied were only spies upon their liberties and constitution.

This principle of liberty, of impatience under restraint, probably proceeds from their happy situation; as they have no foreign foes to distract their attention, every care is fixed upon internal happiness, and as they know no external enemies that are truly dreadful, none can be so great a foe as he who would restrain that freedom of which strangers leave them in quiet possession.

[1] This closely parallels a sentence in the essay on the English character which Goldsmith published in the *Public Ledger*, November 17, 1760 (*Citizen of the World*, Letter XCI): "I know of no country where the influence of climate and soil is more visible than in England, the same hidden cause which gives courage to the dogs and cocks, gives also fierceness to their men" (text of the *Public Ledger*).

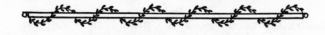

ESSAY VII

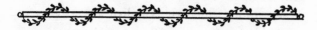

A PREFACE TO A SERIES OF LITERARY ESSAYS[1]

To the Compiler of the PUBLIC LEDGER.

SIR,

THOUGH you expatiate on every other subject; yet in literary news I think your paper
appears defective. The foreign presses teem with
productions that might interest an English reader, and scarce a week passes, but something
curious or useful is published here at home. To
many of your readers an account of such new
publications would be far more entertaining than
a journal of battles or negotiations, an elope-
ment, or a broken leg, the marriage of a celebrated toast, or the adventures of a mad cow.

[1] From the *Public Ledger*, August 19, 1761.

This is the first of a series of eight essays which appeared in the
Ledger between August 19 and September 24, 1761, and of which the
first six are reprinted here. That all eight were the work of the same writer
is shown partly by scattered references throughout the series to the design
announced in the opening paper, but more conclusively by the fact that
each of the essays bears the same signature—a small hand. That this
writer was Goldsmith is established—apart from the parallels to his
acknowledged works pointed out in the notes—by the circumstance that
the last two papers in the series (*Public Ledger*, September 17 and 24)
were reprinted by him, with a few minor corrections, in *Essays by Oliver
Goldsmith* (2d ed., corrected; London: W. Griffin, 1766), pp. 229-40. See
Works, I, 304-10.

The titles given to the essays here do not appear in the *Public Ledger*.

In fact, the reader of a modern news-paper has some right to expect a little refreshment of this nature; we have fought over the German battles even to satiety, Pondicherry and Mocomogo are now our own; it is but just that the same page which is stained with blood and slaughter, should also refresh us with the exertions of benevolence or wisdom; and while it discovers one part of mankind busied in the destruction of the species, it should exhibit the other equally solicitous for their restitution.

I fancy you already perceive that I am only prefacing a design of supplying this defect in your paper for the future. Such I confess is my aim. I intend, with your permission, to furnish the *Ledger* twice a week, with an account of books foreign and domestic, with such other literary news as may contribute to entertain the public, or at least, such as I have found entertaining to myself.

In the execution of a task of this nature neither great abilities nor profound learning will be exerted by the writer, and no great discernment or sagacity will be required on the part of the reader. I could wish that we both brought only our common-sense to the business, and that while I write without pedantry and affectation, he may read with a desire of being pleased. If by this means we can both harmlessly pass over a splenetic hour, the end will be fully answered; to go deeply into the subject is not our design, to please the greatest number we must be superficial; all I intend to offer is a sort of a — — — *stage coach* account of books, we will leave to scholars the painful erudition of a Dyonysius, or the opposing systems of a Bayle.

It is true, that in this design I have been anticipated by many; we have already critics of every size to swarm upon the publications of the day, however I'm determined to add one more to the number, it is better to bite, than be bitten, I shall never stab a reputation for the joke sake; perish the jest which can excite any other sensation than that of a smile.

But I begin to grow tedious; I seldom read the introductory papers of others, and fancy few will read mine; it may not be amiss however to assure those who do, that, to use the common phrase, I shall make up by candour what is wanting in discernment, *I have no connexions to warp my integrity*, nor no enemies to repay; Of the nine hundred and ninety-nine authors with which this city abounds, I dont recollect that I personally know above fifty-seven, thus it is more than eighteen to one, cæteris paribus, that my verdict is always sincere.

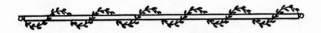

ESSAY VIII

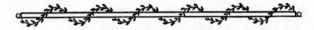

New Fashions in Learning[1]

To the Author of the Public Ledger.

SIR,

IN A week when there are no publications, as at present, I shall content myself with a few remarks as they occur. Before we engage in this literary warfare, therefore, it may not be amiss to take a cursory view of the field of battle, survey the present incitements to learning, or the obstructions which retard its progress.

The power of fashion is not less conspicuous in philosophy than in dress; in this new objects are found to interest curiosity, while the old are quitted as sufficiently explained, or as found unexplicable: A man of letters of the last age should he leave his cell to mix among the scholars of a more modern education, would find himself entirely thrown out from the practised circle of study. About thirty years ago, for instance, no man thought himself learned in nature without being able to account for all its appearances.

[1] From the *Public Ledger*, August 22, 1761.

Scarce one would acknowledge himself ignorant why vapour ascended, and rain fell; why one liquid would dissolve silver, another only gold; or how the water which we drink should pass through such a variety of secretions in so very short a time; every philosopher, chymist, or physician was then ready with his reasons, to account for all these, but now they are acknowledged inextricable; so slow is the progress of science, and time, instead of extending our knowledge, has only encreased our modesty.[1]

To our advantages in this respect we may add, that the connexion between the polite arts and the sciences, is at present closer than formerly; the same man at present is often found eminently to possess a spirit of investigation, and a nice distinguishing taste; how often do we observe united in one, the Wit and the Philosopher; these were formerly separate characters, mutually contemning each other; thus the man of wit was superficial and the philosopher obscure; the one employed his talent to embellish

[1] The same contrast appears in Goldsmith's Introduction to his *Survey of Experimental Philosophy*, first published in 1776, but probably written, at least in part, as early as 1764 (*Works*, V, 149–50): "In the last age it was fashionable to suppose, that we could satisfactorily account for every appearance around us: at present, the real philosopher seems to rest satisfied, that there is much in this science yet to be discovered, and that what he already knows bears no proportion to what remains unknown. He no longer, therefore, pretends to assign causes for all things, but waits till time, industry, or accident, shall bring new lights to guide the enquiry."

folly, the other by his aukward praise made duty disgusting.

But these improvements are common to the learned of Europe in general; the English have some advantages peculiar to themselves. I know no country but this where readers of learning are sufficiently numerous to give every kind of literary excellence adequate encouragement. On whatever subject the philosopher happens to treat, he may be sure of finding an audience numerous enough to reward, and sensible enough to discern his excellence. In other places Princes are obliged to supply this defect; and learning sinks or rises in proportion to royal patronage. A literary King, or a wise Minister, a *Frederic*[1] or a *Colbert* may have promoted knowledge with all the arts of encouragement abroad; but among us we have seen genius spread her broadest pinion under every load that ignorance or vice could lay; and triumph even in the ministry of a *Walpole*.[2]

But whatever alterations or discouragements learning might have undergone, I fancy it will

---

[1] Cf. Goldsmith, *An Enquiry into the Present State of Polite Learning*, chap. v (*Works*, III, 484–86), and "Memoirs of M. de Voltaire" (*Lady's Magazine*, III [November, 1761], 194–97; *Works*, IV, 42–44).

[2] Cf. *An Enquiry into the Present State of Polite Learning* (*Works*, III, 503–4): "But this link [between patronage and literature] now seems entirely broken. Since the days of a certain prime minister, of inglorious memory, the learned have been kept pretty much at a distance."

be readily acknowledged that it was never so useful as at present; there was a time when scholars were the buffoons of a court; they some time after improved into improvers of Princes, but at present every rank of people become their pupils; the meanest mechanic has raised his mind to a desire for knowledge; and the scholar condescends to become his instructor.

We now therefore begin to see the reason why learning assumes an appearance so very different from what it wore some years ago, and that instead of penetrating more deeply into new disquisitions, it only becomes a comment upon the past;[1] the effort is now made to please the multitude, since they may be properly considered as the dispensers of rewards. More pains is taken to bring science down to their capacities, than to raise it beyond its present standard, and his talents are now more useful to society and himself, who can communicate what he knows, than his who endeavours to know more than he can communicate.

[1] Cf. "The Characteristics of Greatness," *Bee*, No. IV, October 27, 1759 (*Works*, II, 374): "This enterprising spirit is, however, by no means the character of the present age: every person who should now leave received opinions, who should attempt to be more than a commentator upon philosophy, or an imitator in polite learning, might be regarded as a chimerical projector"; and *An History of England in a Series of Letters*, II (1764), 141: "All desire of novelty, in thinking, is suppressed amongst us; and our scholars, more pleased with security and ease than honour, cooly follow the reasonings of their predecessors, and walk round the circle of former discovery."

This may account for the number of letters, reviews, magazines, and criticising news-papers, that periodically come from the press; though these performances may justly give a scholar disgust,[1] yet they serve to illuminate the nation. Essay writing, which may be considered as the art of bringing learning from the cell into society, is chiefly encouraged by the multitude; encouragement almost ever produces excellence; among the numbers therefore, who attempt this manner, there are some found to succeed, and this is the only species of writing, in which the present age exceeds the former.

[1] There is a similar passage in *An Enquiry into the Present State of Polite Learning* (*Works*, III, 510–11): "If we turn to either country [France or England], we shall perceive evident symptoms of this natural decay beginning to appear. Upon a moderate calculation, there seems to be as many volumes of criticism published in those countries, as of all other kinds of polite erudition united. Paris sends forth not less than four literary journals every month. . . . . We have two literary reviews in London, with critical news-papers and magazines without number."

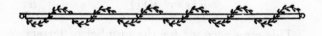

ESSAY IX

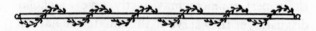

AVENBRUGGER'S DISCOVERY OF PERCUSSION[1]

To the Compiler of the PUBLIC LEDGER.

SIR,

THEY who trust to foreign literary journals for a character of foreign publications will probably be deceived; in them we find every book well written, and every author ingenious; we must consult the works themselves if we would form a just judgment.

As I flatter myself that I shall have many of those publications, almost as soon as the journalists in question, any judgment I am capable of forming, will at least be unbiassed by former authority.

There has been just published at Vienna,[2] a Latin treatise with the following title, "Leopoldi Avenbrugger, Medicinæ Doctoris, in Cæsareo regio nosocomio, nationum Hispanica Medici Ordinarii, inventum novum expercussione thoracis humani ut signo abstrusos interni pectoris

[1] From the *Public Ledger*, August 27, 1761.
[2] The title-page is dated 1761.

64

morbos detegendi: Or, a new invention for the discovery of latent disorders in the breast, by striking the thorax; by Leopold Avenbrugger, M.D. &c."[1]

I have not, says our medical adventurer, been incited to this publication by an itch for writing, nor the delusive pleasure of speculation, but an experience of seven years has confirmed my opinion, and improved my practice in this discovery. He continues to observe, that the thorax (*or that part of the body which lies under the upper ribs and breast bone*) when struck by the tops of the fingers, armed with a glove, sounds somewhat like a drum when covered with a woollen cloth; this sound is in every part pretty nearly equal except just over the heart. In lean men the sound is more perceptible than in fat, and the latter require a stronger blow to excite it. This sound he affirms to be one principal criterion of the state of the thorax, and in those who have a latent disorder there, the difference of sound is easily perceptible.

To examine the patient properly, it is necessary previously to cover the breast with a linen cloth, or to use a glove on the hand which examines; and while the Physician gently taps with

[1] There are two misprints in the title as given here: for "Hispanica" read "Hispanico," and for "expercussione" read "ex percussione." The analysis that follows, though very brief, is in general sufficiently accurate.

his fingers, the patient is to be desired to fetch an inspiration, then to breath, and so forth, till the variation is perfectly perceptible. If the breast be struck, he is to hold his head erect, his shoulders thrown backward; if the side is to be examined, he is to lift both his arms to his head; if his back, then his head is to be bowed forward, and his shoulders drawn down to his breast, by these means the sound will be more distinct and perceptible.

To know the difference between the sounds which the thorax returns when in an healthy state, and when afflicted with any latent internal disorder; let a man first strike his own thorax, and then strike his thigh; and he will perceive that one has an hollow, and the other a kind of dumb fleshy sound; the same difference will appear between an healthy and a disordered breast; the healthy thorax will return the hollow sound described above, the infirm thorax the dumb fleshy sound, generally resembling that of the stricken thigh. To be perfect in this method of distinguishing, the practitioner should examine several breasts, and he will thus be able to discover the minutest deviations. From this method therefore alone, says my author, many disorders may be detected, which it were impossible by any other pathognomonic symptom to discover. For if any particular part of the thorax gives either a more obscure or a louder sound than might be expected, such a difference is probably the result of latent disorder, and the infirmity lies under the part returning that difference of sound. From these premisses confirmed by experience, he has deduced the following observations, 1st, The more fleshy the sound, the more dangerous the disease. 2dly, The greater space of the breast the fleshy sound occupies, the greater the patient's danger. 3dly, If the patient's left side be perceived to be thus affected, it is more dangerous than an affection of the right. 4thly, The upper part of the thorax thus affected, is less dangerous than the lower part. 5thly, The fore part is less dangerous than the hinder part. 6thly, If the whole thorax be deprived of its sound, the symptom is certainly fatal. 7thly, If the breast-bone return no sound, it is fatal. 8thly, If the part which covers the heart returns the fleshy sound, it denotes the death of the patient.

Such are the outlines of this new discovery: whether it may be of use to society or not, there is no necessity for me to pretend to determine, only this may be observed, that the lungs are often even in the most healthy state, found to adhere to the pleura, and in such a case, I fancy

the sound would, in that part, deceive the practitioner; however, I shall not pretend to set my
conjecture against his experience. Upon the
whole, it is a trial that may be easily made, and
to borrow an expression from DOCTOR ROCK,[1] *If
it cannot cure, it can do you no harm.*

I am, Sir, &c.

[1] A well-known quack, whom Goldsmith had twice ridiculed in the
Citizen of the World. See Letters LXVIII (August 25, 1760) and CXIII
(April 14, 1761).

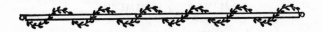

ESSAY X

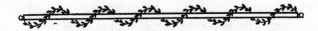

To the Compiler of the PUBLIC LEDGER.

SIR,

IN THIS dearth of publications at home, permit me to travel for literary news abroad, to examine the efforts of other countries in the arts of making life happy, how far they imitate our endeavours for this purpose, and in what particulars they point out to us the way.

Among the kingdoms of Europe which best deserve the wise man's attention, I think Switzerland may be at present placed in the foremost rank; this happy commonwealth equally studious of liberty and improvement, now begins to promote agriculture and commerce; and while other countries imagine themselves acquiring new strength by faithless alliances, or frivolous negotiations, the Switzers are growing truly powerful by encreasing the arts of population;

[1] From the *Public Ledger*, August 29, 1761.

and by giving fertility to those mountains, once the residence of solitary famine.

About three years since there was established at Berne a society for the promotion of agriculture, arts and commerce, probably in imitation of that set up at Stockholm, Dublin, or Florence.[1] The society however at Berne, seems to make a more rapid progress than they, and has already published one volume of transactions, which I have at present before me.[2] From the manner in which it is conducted, we may conceive great hopes of its utility, not only with respect to the country for whose benefit it is written, but the rest of Europe in general. Several persons of great abilities have contributed their assistance, particularly the Marquis de Mirabeau, author of Ami des homes [sic], probably the greatest oeconomical writer now living;[3] yet in fact they seem chiefly obliged to the writers of Great-Britain for almost all their improvements. An Englishman cannot without silent satisfaction see the preference his country re-

---

[1] Goldsmith had praised the work of the Stockholm society in the *Bee*, No. V, November 3, 1759 (*Works*, II, 387). This as well as the other two societies, however, is mentioned in the volume of transactions described in the next note (see I, 15-17).

[2] The full title is *Recueil de memoires, concernants l'oeconomie rurale par une societe etablie a Berne en Suisse.* Tome premier. I. [II.] Partie. Zuric: chez Heidegguer et Compagnie, 1760.

[3] A long memoir by him on agriculture in Switzerland appears in *ibid.*, I, 227-311.

ceives from the rest of mankind for its excellence
in agriculture, the most useful of all arts: they
allow us not only to be the first to promote it
by theory, but to be the most perfect masters
in the practice. Other countries have seen themselves excelled in the very arts they first invent-
ed; we alone can boast of first rationally explain-
ing an art, and then bringing it to perfection.

"The English (say they) were the first to
penetrate into the rich mine of agriculture; and
for a whole age drew forth inexhausted funds
of wealth, before a single nation thought fit to
imitate them.. The last war for the succession of
the house of Austria seemed to awake the attention of Europe. In the course of its devastations
people perceived, that neither the intrigues of
Princes, nor the glittering of courts, nor the
length of cavalcades could give happiness or
security to a people. It was found that to ensure
real respect, real advantages were requisite."
"It was still seen, that wars instead of fixing the
imaginary balance of Europe, only increased its
instability. Those foundations were found uncertain, which a victory might overturn, and
the arts and the commerce of luxury only encreased the enmity of kingdoms, and a desire of
mutual independence. To arrive at this independence, commerce was taught to flourish,

great states began it, and the lesser were obliged to imitate the example."[1]

From some histories recorded in these transactions, we may find almost every country now strug[g]ling for an excellence; the only obstruction those laudable innovators of Berne find in particular, is the attachment of the peasants to their ancient customs and prejudices; when a new art is proposed, the countryman's usual answer is *my father never did so,* and when contrary to his expectation, experience is crowned with success; he cooly observes with a shrug, *I never could have thought it.*[2]

It is both useless and disgusting, to furnish the reader with a syllabus of the contents of this volume; he may find that in the usual indexes to our books of modern husbandry. One or two articles in particular it may not be improper to mention; the first is a method of grafting the walnut-tree;[3] the walnut-tree of the Marquisate du Roiaunois, a little country in the province of Dauphiny in France, is remarkable for the quantity of oil it produces; this tree, which they always graft at home, may be grafted upon any old stock in any other country, and it will produce equally good fruit with that of Riannois.

[1] This paragraph is a free rendering of *Recueil,* I, 14–15.

[2] *Ibid.,* pp. 72–73.   [3] *Ibid.,* pp. 154–59.

The only precaution is, that the scyon must be fresh when grafted.

As we have been frequently of late teized with cures for the bite of a mad dog,[1] it may be attended with ridicule to mention still one more; However the authenticity of that I am going to mention,[2] which is attested by numbers, and they of the first distinction, may serve at once for my encouragement and excuse. The herb Anagallis or Pimpernel is said to be a most effectual remedy for this terrible calamity, this herb gathered in July, suffered to dry, and pulverized, may be given in quantity of half a drachm to that of a drachm, in a simple distilled water of the same plant or in tea. After which the patient is to fast for two hours. One dose is generally sufficient, however it may be repeated in eight or ten hours after with safety.

I am, &c.

[1] Numerous such "cures" had been printed in the *Public Ledger*, as well as in other journals, during the height of the mad-dog panic of the summer of 1760. See Gibbs's note in *Works*, III, 260. Goldsmith had contributed two satirical letters dealing with the subject to the *Ledger* in August of that year. See *Citizen of the World*, Letter LXIX (August 29), and especially the following from Letter LXVIII (August 25): "The English . . . . have one doctor for the eyes, another for the toes; they have their sciatica doctors and inoculating doctors; they have one doctor who is modestly content with securing them from bug bites, and five hundred who prescribe for the bite of a mad dog" (text of the *Public Ledger*). Cf. also *The Vicar of Wakefield*, chap. xx (*Works*, I, 159).

[2] *Recueil*, I, 213–21.

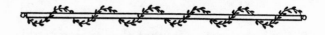

ESSAY XI

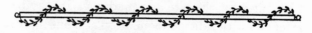

South American Giants[1]

To the Compiler of the Public Ledger.

SIR,

THE instability of philosophic systems has long been a subject of ridicule or complaint; innovations in the subjects of taste or religion are more permanent; but almost every age produces new attempts to explain the secrets of nature, as some latent property happens to be known, so that the old man finds the system of his youth exploded or forgotten.

Among other disquisitions in physic or natural history, that of the size of men in different countries or different ages has not a little employed speculation, and produced disputes.[2] On one side the testimony of all antiquity which mentions giants as familiarly known; the skeletons dug up of a monstrous size, and some more modern discoveries in the Southern parts of

[1] From the *Public Ledger*, September 5, 1761.

[2] There is an extended discussion of this question in Goldsmith's *History of the Earth and Animated Nature*, II (1774), 258–65.

America, are brought to confirm their existence. On the other side, when these proofs come to be examined, the ancients will appear frequently to have been deceived themselves, or to have attempted to deceive others, the skeletons will appear to have belonged to other animals, never to men, and the existence of the tall Patagons in Southern America has been called into question by Sir Hans Sloane, Frazer, and others.[1] In this manner the controversy seemed almost at an end, but there has been lately published at Madrid a work, entituled, Giganthalogia, by P. Joseph Tarrubia,[2] proving the existence of this species of men, not only from the concurrent testimony of all antiquity in this our old world; but from several Indian antiquities discoverable in the new. The monstrous statues of several of their idols which are affirmed to have been no bigger than the life, and several utensils that from their size could have been made use of only by giants, are confirmations of this; but what is a more irrefragable proof than either, the author insists upon having seen several Spaniards, who

---

[1] Cf. Buffon, *Histoire naturelle*, III (1749), 508-9.

[2] The book referred to is probably José Torrubia's *Aparato para la historia natural española* (Madrid, 1754), Section X of which (pp. 54-79) bears the title "Gigantologia española." There is an account of the controversy over the size of men, with an incidental mention of the arguments of Torrubia, in the Abbé de Pauw's *Recherches philosophiques sur les Américains*, I (Berlin, 1768), 281-326.

have seen those monstrous men as they happened to stray from their wild retreats, verging towards the straits of Magellan. They are described as being nine or ten feet high; strong in proportion to their size; and active to a surprising degree, but instead of dipping into a controversy, that time and not disputations will one day determine,[1] I shall only transcribe a story told us of one of those extraordinary species of beings.[2]

Madalena de Niqueza was one of those unhappy women, who leaving Europe, expected to find affluence and fortune in some of the extensive provinces, subject to the Spanish monarchy in Southern America. Those who are friendless at home are generally friendless among stran-

---

[1] Cf. *An History of the Earth and Animated Nature*, II (1774), 258: "Some have affirmed the probability of such a race [of giants]; and others, as warmly have denied the possibility of their existence. But it is not from any speculative reasonings, upon a subject of this kind, that information is to be obtained; it is not from the disputes of the scholar, but the labours of the enterprising, that we are to be instructed in this enquiry." A later passage in the same work indicates that Goldsmith was convinced of the reality of the Patagonian giants. After summarizing Magellan's account, he goes on (II, 261–62): "This account, with a variety of other circumstances, has been confirmed by succeeding travellers. . . . . The last voyager we have had, that has seen this enormous race, is Commodore Byron. I have talked with the person who first gave the relation of that voyage, and who was the carpenter of the Commodore's ship; he was a sensible, understanding man, and I believe extremely faithful. By him, therefore, I was assured, in the most solemn manner, of the truth of his relation; and this account has since been confirmed by one or two publications; in all which the particulars are pretty nearly the same."

[2] I have been unable to discover the source of this story. It does not appear in the work by Torrubia mentioned above, p. 75, n. 2.

gers. She wandered for some time in the streets of Carthagena, feeling all the misery of houseless ind[i]gence, and an unfavourable sky. In this forlorn state an Indian shepherd saw, married her, and brought her with him to his native village, which bordered on the savage countries of the Guanoas and Chiquitos.

Those barbarous nations which could never be reduced to the subjection of the Spaniards, make continual excursions upon the countries that have been reduced, and kill and carry away the inhabitants who happen to fall into their power. In one of these incursions Madalena and her husband were taken prisoners and carried some hundred leagues to the south, where they were several times exchanged for other commodities in the usual course of traffic, till at length they arrived among a people still if possible more rude than their former masters, and here they were put to their usual employment of keeping cattle.

In this situation, however, they had not long continued, when a general alarm was spread thro' the Indian town where they were stationed, for an army of Giants were marching forward, and laying all things waste with fire and sword before them. Madalena could perceive, that the Indians instead of attempting to fly, rather endeavoured to conceal themselves, as they despaired of finding safety by swiftness, in which the Giants so much excelled them. The formidable army at length appeared, but instead of spreading that terror which was expected, she was surprized to see the humanity with which they treated their prisoners. This body of Giants consisted of about four hundred, the lowest soldier in the whole army was not under nine feet high; and the tallest was about eleven. Their features were regular, their limbs exactly proportioned; they had a sweetness and affability in their looks, and their speech was deep, clear, and sonorous. Madalena and her husband were now made prisoners once more, but treated with infinitely more compassion and tenderness than by their former masters. The Gyant to whose lot she fell used to hearken to the account of her adventures with pleasure, and seemed to regard her misfortunes with a passion mixed with love and pity. They lived in a state of perfect equality among each other, and had people of ordinary stature to do the domestic offices of life. Their women were by no means proportionably large, not being above six feet and an half high, and the children when brought into the world were of the usual size. In this situation Madalena continued for almost four years, when growing weary of servitude, she was resolved to travel down to the Western shore, which bounds the great pacific ocean, which she affected [*sic*], and was brought off by a Spanish bark and carried to Panama, from whence some time after she found means of returning to Europe.

I am, &c.

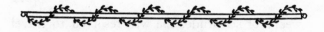

ESSAY XII

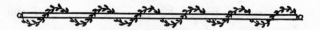

THE TASTE FOR SHOWS AND PROCESSIONS DEPLORED[1]

To the Compiler of the PUBLIC LEDGER.

SIR,

WHEN I undertook the task of reviewing in your paper every thing that appeared, twice a week, I never considered, whether there would be publications enough to keep me going. At present, though I keep a pretty sharp look out, yet scarce any thing occurs, except Companions to the Coronation, or Guides to the Coronation, not forgetting the pretty poesy for the Coronation Ring, with all which I confess myself a perfect stranger. I scarce know Garter King at Arms by sight; and the Champion of England, who is soon to challenge all mankind, may be a giant or a pigmy, for aught I can tell.[2]

It is happy however for the nation, that such shews and processions seldom arrive, and the

---

[1] From the *Public Ledger*, September 10, 1761.

[2] Cf. the allusions to Garter King at Arms and the Champion in *Citizen of the World*, Letter CV (February 10, 1761).

only motive that can induce me to pardon the eagerness of my countrymen on the present occasion, is the infrequency of it. Such sights seldom improve a nation. "The luxury of repeated triumphal processions," says a Roman historian, "at length subdues the conquerors themselves." The gay frippery exhibited on such occasions turns the mind of the spectator to false objects of admiration, and induces him to prefer finery to happiness.

A city when at length debauched into a love of processions and cavalcades, for such passions encrease by indulgence, loses all its manly severity, and every incentive to true glory. Under such a government, not the nobleman who thinks best, but who cuts the finest figure will meet with most respect; the contest will be not who can do his country most service, but who shall have the greatest number of mameluks and train-bearers at his heels, the external figure shall denominate the man, and glory be founded in the shout of a mob.

It was said of Lucullus, that whenever he had a fancy to do a man a prejudice, he made him a present of fine cloaths; this he found, by experience, effectually to contaminate the mind of the receiver, and to render him either effeminate or venal, ready to receive a bribe to support this finery, or too cowardly to oppose usurpation; a kingdom may be compared to a single individual in this respect, and when no arts are encouraged but the arts of luxury, every mind will be set upon trifles, the inhabitants must necessarily degenerate, till all at last, like the modern Italians, they seem castrated at a single blow.

When I turn my eyes to modern Italy, that country of cavalcade, pageant, and frippery, their excesses in this respect, in some measure excite my pitty and contempt. Their passion for finery is in general in a reciprocal proportion to the beggary of the state. To think of cities laying out immense sums in adorning a temple of pasteboard, while their very walls are actually falling to ruin.[1] To think of triumphal entries passing through those towns who never knew any but their own conquerors; such considerations must in the present scene of things excite a concern at the dreaded effects of misplaced admiration at home, and that such shews may produce more than a transient inconvenience.

[1] With this cf. the description of Italy in the first edition (1759) of Goldsmith's *Enquiry into the Present State of Polite Learning* (*Works*, III, 481–82): "Happy country, where the pastoral age begins to revive!—where the wits even of Rome, are united into a rural group of nymphs and swains, under the appellation of modern Arcadians!—where, in the midst of porticos, processions, and cavalcades, abbés turned shepherds, and shepherdesses without sheep, indulge their innocent *divertimenti!* Perhaps, while I am writing, a shepherdess of threescore is listening to the pastoral tale of a French abbé: a warm imagination might paint her in all the splendour of ripened beauty, reclining on a pasteboard rock; might

The Spanish monarchy found, that when a taste for magnificence was once introduced into that kingdom, no sumptuary laws they could enact were sufficient to eradicate the evil. They had by their own authority first invited the people into a passion for shews and magnificent entries; the slightest conquest was attended with a solemn procession; their very defeats in Holland furnished out the pageantry of triumphs at home: the people were pleased at the shew, imitated their betters, as far as they were able, and at length became fine, and proud, and beggarly. But this has been the case in every state; Ministers and Governors first teach their subjects the arts of luxurious necessity, and then by sumptuary laws are obliged to constrain the consequences which have resulted from their own example.

But I am not for inveighing against the

---

fancy her lover, with looks inexpressibly tender, ravishing a kiss from the snowy softness of one of her hands, while the other holds a crook according to pastoral decorum. Amidst such frippery as this, there was no place for friendless Metastasio; he has left Italy, and the genius of nature seems to have left it with him." Still closer is the description of modern Italy in *The Traveller*, especially ll. 145–52 (I quote the text of the first edition):

"Yet, though to fortune lost, here still abide
Some splendid arts, the wrecks of former pride;
From which the feeble heart and long fall'n mind
An easy compensation seem to find.
Here may be seen, in bloodless pomp array'd,
The paste-board triumph and the cavalcade;
Processions form'd for piety and love,
A mistress or a saint in every grove."

universal pleasure of the people at present, I would only endeavour to bound its effects. I would only endeavour to persuade the few who chuse to think upon this occasion, that the fewer shews we have of this kind, it must be so much the better; that glaring trifles are ever apt to wean the mind from more important pursuits; I would not willingly be the only gloomy creature in this universal scene of festivity. I could however, wish to find men, when employed upon trifles, conscious that they are but trifles; I would have it understood, that all the importance which the *vulgar* great are apt to arrogate from such distinctions, only secures the admiration of folly.

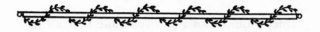

ESSAY XIII

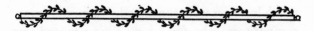

SIR,

YOU demanded what public rewards the learned in this country receive, or what employments in the state are set apart for their administration. Know then, my friend, that they receive none. It is here the general opinion that polite literature by giving too liberal a turn to the mind, disqualifies men from going through the drudgery of an office. When once a man addicts himself to the sciences, or commences author, if he be not of the church, his friends

[1] From the *Lady's Magazine*, III (September, 1761), 110–12. Aside from the style and turn of humor, which seem to me distinctly characteristic, the evidence for Goldsmith's authorship of this essay is mainly circumstantial. Its subject—rewards for genius in England—was one of his stock themes: he had treated it at length in his *Enquiry into the Present State of Polite Learning* in 1759 (*Works*, III, 500–509) and had touched upon it briefly in the *Citizen of the World* in 1760 and 1761 (see especially Letters XIII, LVII, and XCIII). Moreover, at the time the essay appeared in the *Lady's Magazine* he was himself the editor of that periodical (see above, p. xxxii) and a regular contributor to its pages; the September number, for example, opened with an instalment of his "Memoirs of M. de Voltaire," and in addition contained a reprint of an essay which he had published in the *Public Ledger*, September 24. This evidence of course is far from conclusive, but it is perhaps sufficient to justify the inclusion of the essay in this collection.

lament him as lost, and conclude that all pains taken to save him from ruin will be fruitless. An ingenious gentleman of my acquaintance, solicited for a place in a public office, where much business was transacted. There were many competitors, who for a long time opposed him, but without much hopes of success, till at length one of them succeeded by maliciously insinuating that my friend was a scholar, a man of genius and the author of a celebrated work.

But projectors in particular meet with the least favour. If one of them should be so unfortunate as to invent or discover something highly conducive to the happiness and welfare of mankind, he would certainly be ruined. His merciless creditors would throw him into a goal for the debts which he contracted for the public good. There he perishes unpitied by his fellow-citizens, who enjoy in tranquility the fruits of his discoveries.

About two hundred years since, Sir Hugh Middleton, an ingenious gentleman, formed a river by collecting some streams together, and then brought it thro' a long tract of country to this metropolis;[1] by which a great part of the inhabitants are supplied with water at a cheap

[1] On Middleton see Smollett, *A Complete History of England* (3d ed.; London, 1759), VII, 99 n.

rate. When his project was near compleated, his credit failed, and his creditors confined him in a goal as if he had been guilty of an enormous crime. After six months imprisonment, queen Elizabeth procured his release, but he never enjoyed the benefit of his own scheme.

The ingenious inventor of the machine for weaving of stockings was forced to earn his livelihood in a strange country, by discovering his invention to foreigners, which if kept secret at home, had been the source of great wealth to this nation.

The first projector of cross posts, by which the communication between the distant provinces is facilitated, was ruined.

There has lately appeared a projector, one of whose schemes is more beneficial to mankind than all the others added together. He proposes to tan human hides, and has shewn the vast advantages which will accrue to mankind from this project in every point of view. I have sent you his treatise translated into Italian, it is addressed to a society of gentlemen who have incorporated themselves for the encouragement of arts, manufactures and commerce.[1] If this proj-

[1] The Society for the Encouragement of Arts, Manufactures, and Commerce had been in existence since 1754. Several of Goldsmith's friends, including Newbery, Grainger, and Johnson, were members at the time this essay was published, and he himself was to become a mem-

ect had been presented to his holiness the Pope, the author would have been advanced into the highest rank of the learned, and have perhaps found a place at the Conclave. I have not as yet heard that his Britannic Majesty has settled a pension on the author, in question, nor that the parliament will take his scheme into consideration, nor that the society have presented him their thanks, nor that a statue has been erected to his honour. He must wait till posterity gives approbation to his designs, and he may receive applause when it can be of service no longer.[1]

I am, dear Sir, &c.

---

ber on November 17, 1762 (MS Minutes under that date, and Register of Members). He is said to have been a candidate for the secretaryship in 1760 (see Thomas Davies, *Memoirs of the Life of David Garrick, Esq.* [new ed.; London, 1780], II, 143–44). It is impossible to verify this story, for his name does not appear in the list of candidates whose petitions, according to the MS Minutes, were presented to the Society on March 12 and again on March 19 of that year.

[1] Cf. *Citizen of the World*, Letter XCIII (January 7, 1761): ". . . . you have seen like me many literary reputations promoted by the influence of fashion, which have scarce survived the possessor; you have seen the poor hardly earn the little reputation they acquired, and their merit only acknowledged when they were incapable of enjoying the pleasures of popularity. . . . ." In a somewhat similar vein are the remarks of the "man in black" on Pope in Letter XIII (February 25, 1760).

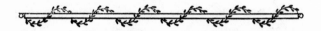

ESSAY XIV

THOUGHTS UPON THE PRESENT SITUATION OF
AFFAIRS[1]

THOUGH I seldom indulge myself in political speculations, yet the continuance of the
present war,[2] and the late revolutions of the
ministry[3] would call for even weakness itself to
rejoice or to deplore in the general concern. It
was a maxim in one of the states of Greece that

[1] From the *Lady's Magazine*, III (October, 1761), 150–52, where it
immediately follows an instalment of the "Memoirs of M. de Voltaire."
  That Goldsmith wrote this essay there can, I think, be little doubt.
It is not so much that it expresses a general attitude which, as will be
seen from the following notes, had been consistently his since 1759 and
which he was to reiterate in later works, for "anti-imperialism" of the type
found here, though far from the dominant view, had of course other ex-
ponents among English journalists during these years. The really conclusive considerations are, first, the numerous definite parallels to Goldsmith's known writings, both earlier and later, which the essay presents
—parallels of precisely the same kind as those discussed in the Introduction (see above, pp. xxii–xxviii)—and, second, the fact that it appeared
as an editorial pronouncement (this is shown by the absence of the
usual mark of a contributed article, the formal address to the editor)
in a magazine of which Goldsmith, disguised as the "Honourable Mrs.
Caroline Stanhope," was at the time in charge.

[2] The negotiations for a peace with France which had been under
way since July were broken off late in September, shortly before this
essay was published (see "The History of the Present War," *Annual
Register for the Year 1761*, pp. 22, 41).

[3] The resignation of Pitt is announced in the same issue of the *Lady's
Magazine* (see III, 187, 189, 190–91).

none, not even women should sit unconcerned in the calamities or threatened dangers of their country. For my part I would advise my own sex[1] in the same manner to shew a becoming concern for the public, provided they give way neither to violence, nor affectation. I think it a duty becoming us, whose greatest power is exerted in peace, to wish for its return. In imitation of our great queen, I could eagerly desire to see the sword sheathed, and our brothers, fathers, husbands, children, returned in safety. To protract the war may bring perhaps an accession of wealth, or honour; but I doubt whether it can add new happiness.

The empire of England now happily finds itself in the most glorious circumstances it has hitherto ever experienced; more formidable abroad, and more powerful at home. The conjuncture is decisive in its favour, and if its negotiations do not complete what its arms have begun, they are lost for ever.

But while we see and enjoy our present successes, we should prudently consider them as glorious, only because likely to be productive of a lasting peace; that is the reward of all our fatigue, and if we have that with security and honour, every end of war is answered. I must

[1] The speaker is of course the ostensible editor, "Mrs. Stanhope."

own, that I have with great pleasure observed their Britannic and Prussian majesties former declarations, in which they testify their desire of re-establishing the tranquillity of Europe, and bringing on a general peace. I cannot without admiration think that we have ministers, who in the midst of success, and surrounded with conquest and glory, should still so far prefer the interests of mankind to their own as to make the first propositions.

But while we applaud their sagacity, let us not encrease their difficulties, by expecting more advantageous terms of peace, (if there should be a congress for that purpose) than is consistent with the honour of our enemies to give, than is consistent with our own security to accept. The greater our expectations, the greater difficulty will our ministers find in bringing the enemy to terms, by this means the wish'd-for peace will be protracted, and the rest left to the event of uncertain success.[1]

[1] Cf. Goldsmith's essay in the *Busy Body*, No. VI, October 20, 1759 (*Works*, IV, 467): "It is but prolonging the wished-for peace, to prescribe such terms as is consistent neither with the interest nor the honour of our enemies to accept. It is but rendering us ridiculous, to expect such terms as we can never compel them to"; and his *Political View of the Result of the Present War with America*, a fragment written in 1760 or the early part of 1761 and known, since it was first printed by Prior in 1837, under the misleading title of the *Preface and Introduction to the History of the Seven Years' War* (on the history of this piece see K. C. Balderston, *A Census of the Manuscripts of Oliver Goldsmith* [New York, 1926], pp. 38–39): "We may, however, upon this occasion be permitted to remark that, as peace is the end of war, it is extremely injurious to the govern-

There is not a more certain maxim in politics, than that a peace bought too dear can never last long; it is the part therefore of a victorious people to give up something of its advantages, and to soften their enemies dishonour, with such terms as may keep them content with their situation.

There is another maxim, which experience has ever testified the truth of; I mean, that an empire, by too great a foreign power may lessen its natural strength, and that dominion often becomes more feeble as it grows more extensive.[1] The ancient Roman empire is a strong instance of the truth of the assertion; one of their emperors perceived too late its natural weakness, but could not attempt to lessen it, as that would be an indication of the motive of his fears. The

---

ment to render a peace difficult, by prescribing impracticable conditions, by teaching the multitude to expect concessions from the enemy which every reasonable being knows our enemies cannot be compelled to make . . . ." (*Works*, V, 32). This last passage does not appear in the article on "The Present Crisis of Europe and America" (*Literary Magazine*, III [July, 1758], 289–92), from which its immediate context in the *Political View* was largely derived.

[1] Cf. *Citizen of the World*, Letter XVII (March 13, 1760): "The best English politicians, however, are sensible, that to keep their present conquests, would be rather a burthen than an advantage to them, rather a diminution of their strength than an encrease of power. It is in the politic as in the human constitution; if the limbs grow too large for the body, their size, instead of improving, will diminish the vigour of the whole"; and Letter XXV (April 1, 1760): "Happy, very happy might they have been, had they known when to bound their riches and their glory. Had they known that extending empire is often diminishing power . . . ." (*Public Ledger* text). The same idea is also developed in *An History of England in a Series of Letters*, II (1764), 241–42, 254.

Ottoman power at present, as a late ingenious writer has observed, is one of the most extensive, yet perhaps one of the most feeble empires in the world;[1] is it not possible for England to have colonies too large for her natural power to manage? Of this we may be very sure, the more powerful her colonies become, the less obedient will they be to another's power.[2]

There is still a third maxim, which I would beg leave to repeat on this occasion; I mean, that a country may be very wretched and very successful; resembling a lighted taper, which the brighter it blazes, only consumes the faster.[3] Sweden is, perhaps, as strong an instance of this truth, as history can shew. In the very midst of the victories of its romantic monarch, never

[1] Cf. *Citizen of the World*, Letter XVII (March 13, 1760): ". . . . thus subordination is destroyed, and a country is swallowed up in the extent of its own dominions. The Turkish empire would be more formidable, were it less extensive. Were it not for those countries, which it can neither command, nor give entirely away, which it is obliged to protect, but from which it has no power to enforce obedience" (*Public Ledger* text).

[2] Cf. *ibid.*: "The colonies should always bear an exact proportion to the mother country; when they grow populous, they grow powerful, and by becoming powerful, they become independent. . . . ."

[3] There is an approximation to this image in the *Busy Body*, No. VI, October 20, 1759 (*Works*, IV, 467): "It is very possible for a country to be very victorious and very wretched. . . . . A country at war resembles a flambeaux; the brighter it burns, the sooner it is often wasted." It was to recur in *The Traveller*, ll. 399–400:

> "Have we not . . . .
> Seen all her triumphs but destruction haste,
> Like flaring tapers brightening as they waste; . . . . ?"

was there so wretched a nation seen; without money that would pass out of their own dominions, without trade, and even without content.[1] Let us not build too much upon our present successes, while there is even a possibility of a reverse; let us be content with a lasting, rather than a triumphant peace, and expect no more from our ministers at the conclusion of it, than security and indemnification.

Indemnification for what is past, and security for the future, are the essential objects in a treaty of pacification, but both these may be easily effected without any accession to our present dominions; and, instead of draining our

[1] The illustration of Sweden occurs in the essay in the *Busy Body* quoted in the preceding note (*Works*, IV, 467): "The victories of Sweden have oppressed that people so much as to render them quite insignificant in the political scale of Europe ever since." It is probable that this observation on Sweden was inspired by the following passage in Justus Van Effen's *Relation d'un voyage de Hollande en Suede*, a work which Goldsmith is known to have utilized in October, 1759, in two numbers of the *Bee* (see *Modern Language Review*, VIII [1913], 319–22): "Mettez-vous dans l'esprit, Monsieur, un Royaume, qui par lui-même, n'est pas extrêmement riche, engagé dans une cruelle guerre de plus de vingt années; guerre qui couta beaucoup dans ses heureux commencemens, & qui exigea une dépense infiniment plus grande vers la fin, lorsque les défaites y furent aussi suivies que les victoires l'avoient été d'abord. Figurez-vous cette guerre conduite par un Prince absolu & despotique, à qui le dernier sol de ses Sujets étoit acquis, comme la dernière goute de leur sang. Ajoutez-y un Roi éloigné de ses Etats pendant plusieurs années, & les desordres qu'une si triste absence devoit traîner après elle. Ce n'est pas tout: un déréglement universel dans les Finances devoit par une triste nécessité découler de toutes ces causes réunies, aussi-bien qu'une suspension absolue du Commerce, qui s'écarte naturellement des pays où l'argent est rare. Mais quand il y auroit eu encore quelque moyen de soutenir un peu ce Commerce, il étoit impossible de le mettre en œuvre" (*Œuvres diverses* [Amsterdam, 1742], II, 468–69).

natural country by peopling new acquisitions abroad, better it were could we abridge the enemy's power at home.

I suppose, it is now seen at what I aim; the keeping the French down to a certain strength at sea, to a stipulated number of ships of war, would give us security; and the restitution of Minorca, and the re-establishing our allies in their power, a sufficient indemnification.

To be as explicit as possible, I see no reason why we should aggrandize our colonies at our own expence; an acquisition of new colonies is useless, unless they are peopled; but to people those desarts that lie behind our present colonies, would require multitudes from the mother-country; and I do not find we are too populous at home. All that are willing or able to work in England whether men or women, can live happy, and those who are neither able nor willing, would starve on the banks of the Ohio, as well as in the streets of St. Giles's; it is not the lazy or the maimed that are wanted to people colonies abroad, but the healthy and industrious, and such members of society, I think, would be more usefully kept at home.[1] To enlarge our

[1] Cf. *Citizen of the World*, Letter XVII (March 13, 1760): "Yet, obvious as these truths are, there are many Englishmen who are for transplanting new colonies, for peopling the desarts of America with the refuse of their countrymen, and (as they express it) the waste of an

territories therefore in America, should not be
the aim of our ministry, but to secure those we
are already in possession of: but perhaps an op-
ponent will say, if we people those countries, we
shall have more tobacco, more hemp, and we
shall be able to procure prodigious quantities of
raw silk! away then with thousands of our best
and most useful inhabitants, that we may be
furnished with tobacco and raw silk; send our
honest tradesmen and brave soldiers to people
those desolate regions, that our merchants may
furnish Europe with tobacco and raw silk.[1]

exuberant nation. And who are those unhappy creatures who are to be
thus sent over? Not the sickly, for they are unwelcome guests abroad as
well as at home; nor the idle, for they would starve as well behind the
Appalachian mountains as in the streets of this metropolis. This refuse
is composed of the laborious and enterprising, of men who can be service-
able to their country at home . . . ." (*Public Ledger* text).

[1] Cf. *Citizen of the World*, Letter XVII, immediately following the
passage quoted in the last note: "And what are the commodities which
this colony when establish'd, are to produce in return? Raw silk, hemp,
and tobacco. England, therefore, must make an exchange of her best
and bravest subjects for raw silk, hemp, and tobacco; their hardy
veterans, and honest tradesmen must be truck'd for a box of snuff or
a silk petticoat" (text of the *Public Ledger*). The germ of this development, repeated in such closely similar terms in 1760 and 1761, is perhaps
to be found in the *Literary Magazine* (I [October, 1756], 298–99), in a
review, ascribed to Johnson by Boswell (see *Life of Johnson* [ed. Hill;
Oxford, 1887], I, 309), of Lewis Evans's *Geographical, Historical, Political,
Philosophical and Mechanical Essays*: "We have at home more land than
we cultivate, and more materials than we manufacture; by proper regula-
tions we may employ all our people, and give every man his chance of
rising to the full enjoyment of all the pleasures and advantages of a
civilised and learned country. I know not indeed, whether we can at home
procure any great quantity of *raw silk*, which we are told is to be had in
so great plenty upon the banks of the *Ohio*. Away therefore with thousands and millions to those dreadful desarts, that we may no longer want
raw silk. Who that had not often observed how much one train of thought

Though I have seen such sordid opinions broached from the press, yet I hope our present glorious ministry will not comply with the mercenary or the vulgar in this respect; we are a commercial nation, it is true, but that is our smallest glory; we have excelled in arts and arms, Europe owns our superiority; let us not then sacrifice every consideration to commerce alone, and while we have of late carried on such a glorious war, let us not conclude a peace dictated by avarice or mistaken policy.

---

sometimes occupies the mind could think so wild a project seriously proposed." That Goldsmith was familiar in 1760 with the volume of the *Literary Magazine* in which this article appeared has been shown by John W. Oliver (*Times Literary Supplement*, May 18, 1922, p. 324).

ESSAY XV

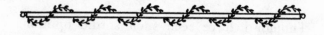

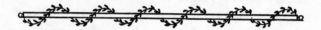

THE INDIGENT PHILOSOPHER
Numb. 1. The Author's Motives
for Writing[1]

I HAVE just come from being the only mourn-
er at the funeral of my old friend Sir William
Abner. He was buried in Bunhill-Fields at the
expence of the parish, and the Sexton and I saw
him decently laid in his grave. There is a luxury
in sorrow when it is all our own; so that I gave
an indulgence to mine upon this occasion. I considered myself as the only person upon earth

[1] From *Lloyd's Evening Post, and British Chronicle*, January 20–22,
1762, where it forms the first of a series of four essays, all printed in the
"Postscript." Goldsmith's authorship of the series is established by both
internal and external evidence. The internal evidence taken by itself is
perhaps conclusive only for the third essay. The external evidence, however, would appear to remove all doubts. It consists of two facts: (1)
that the whole of the fourth essay (February 8–10) was acknowledged
by Goldsmith, who reprinted it in 1765 in *Essays by Mr. Goldsmith*
(see *Works*, I, 259–62, where it bears the title, "Specimen of a Magazine in Miniature"), and (2) that a long passage from the second
essay was incorporated by him into the text of another paper in the same
collection, the greater part of which had originally appeared in the *Busy
Body* (see below, p. 104, n. 3). The only question is whether the four essays
were originally written for *Lloyd's Evening Post*. The reference in the
second essay to the man at the club who had been reading about the Cock-
Lane Ghost in the *Ledger* may possibly point to that paper, a file of which
for 1762 seems unfortunately to be nowhere available, as the place of
original publication. On the other hand, in Numb. 4, in a passage some-

that was grieved for his loss. He had long been
cut off from the social world. His improvidence
had rendered him miserably poor, his integrity
had banished him from the company of the
needy like himself, and he long lived in this town
an Hermit in the midst of society.

I attended him, as his Friend and Physician,
during his last illness. I soon saw that he was
dying, and I was glad of it. He was leaving a
world unfit for him, and I felt some satisfaction
from that motive, though grieved that I was
going to lose the only friend and companion I
had. "My honest Charles (said he to me, as I
sate by his bed side), we have been friends in the
worst of times, and I now thank you for it; we
have helped to support our load of misery as
well as we could together; but I am now weary
of my part of the burden, and am well pleased
that I am going to lay it down; you must bear
the rest alone as well as you can; but you see,
by my success in life, that neither abilities, nor

---

what altered in the version included in the *Essays*, Goldsmith says: "I
shall hop from subject to subject, and, if properly encouraged, I intend
in time to adorn Lloyd's Postscript with pictures" (see also above,
p. xxxiii).

The title of the series was probably suggested by that of Marivaux'
periodical, *L'Indigent philosophe*, from which Goldsmith had adapted his
"Adventures of a Strolling Player" (*British Magazine*, I [October, 1760],
577–82). See A. L. Sells, *Les sources françaises de Goldsmith* (Paris,
1924), pp. 76–79. The titles of the individual essays I have taken from the
Index to the bound volume of *Lloyd's Evening Post*, January–June, 1762.

virtue, nor even a title, are of any great service for present happiness without prudence and perseverance.[1] When I ceased to set a proper value upon myself, the world began to despise me; they mistook my modesty for want of merit, and gave their esteem and relief to those who had the bravery and the assurance to arrogate them as their due. Believe me, Charles, that to aim at something much above us, is almost to deserve the object of our aim."[2]

Such was the situation of this poor man; nor, except in the name alone, has fancy had any part in the picture. By dropping from his sphere in life when young, through a faulty timidity, his spirits, by degrees, shrunk with his circumstances, till he was at last deprived of every thing worth desiring here, or capable of retarding his stay.

But how are his advice and example lost upon me, who now, with his catastrophe in view, sit

---

[1] A frequent theme in Goldsmith. See *Citizen of the World*, Letter VI (February 1, 1760): "You see, my dearest friend, what imprudence has brought thee to: from opulence, a tender family, surrounding friends, and your master's esteem, it has reduced thee to want, persecution, and, still worse, to our mighty monarch's displeasure. Want of prudence is too frequently the want of virtue . . . ."; *The Life of Richard Nash* (1762): " . . . . she remains the strongest instance to posterity, that want of prudence alone almost cancels every other virtue" (*Works*, IV, 98); and the title of chap. xxviii of *The Vicar of Wakefield* (first published in 1766, but probably completed during 1762; see below, p. 117, n. 1): "Happiness and misery rather the result of prudence than of virtue in this life."

[2] Cf. the *Bee*, No. IV, October 27, 1759 (*Works*, II, 374).

down to write in a News-Paper *for bread*. Dropping from my sphere to this most humble method of all literary exhibition: Alas! how ill do I support the dignity of a Scholar or a Gentleman, by thus consigning my little acquirements to the same vehicle that must too often necessarily convey insipidity and ignorance! How cold a reception must every effort receive that comes thus endeavouring to regulate the passions, in a place where almost every paragraph tends to excite them; where readers of taste seldom seek for gratification; and where readers of politicks and news seldom require more than the objects of their peculiar curiosity.

But I must write, or I cannot live. Tho' modesty, tho' indolence and love of obscurity would conspire to dissuade me, I must, perhaps, for life, incur the reproach of venality. I must be thought an hireling if I receive small retribution for attempting to instruct society; while others escape the censure, though they receive immense fortunes for this purpose, without scarce an effort to instruct themselves.[1] But let folly or dullness join to brand me; I shall take no shame to myself for endeavouring to enforce morals or improve good humour. There is no shame in

[1] There is a slight resemblance here to *Citizen of the World*, Letter LVII (July 9, 1760).

making truth wear the face of entertainment, or
letting ridicule fly only at mental deformity;
nor is there any shame in being paid for it.
It is not every scholar who pretends to despise
this prostitution of talents, whose works have
sufficient beauty to allure our employer to pro-
pose terms of similar prostitution. It is not
every Gentleman who can forego, like me, the
common and vendible topicks of government
abuse, on which I could descant perhaps with
elegance, in order to select general follies; on
which topick it is probable I may be generally
disregarded. There is no merit, nor do I claim
any in the benevolence of my present publication; but there is at least some in the selection
of my subject: And shall I be ashamed of being
paid a trifle for doing this, when Bishops are
paid for scarce preaching on Sundays! Shall I be
ashamed of doing this! This power, if I have any
power, was the only patrimony I received from
a poor father! And shall I be ashamed of this!
*By Heavens I more glory in it, than if possessed
of all the wealth that ever fortune threw on fools.*

But to be more simple, let it at present be
sufficient to observe, that tho' Indigence be my
motive for this publication, yet I have taken
Honesty for my guide: I am one of those characters who being always poor, have been ever

receiving advice from their friends and acquaint-ance. As it has been administered to me in doses of every size, I intend, for the benefit of these good advising friends, in this public manner to dose them with part of it back. To give advice may do me some good, for I solemnly protest I was never benefited by taking theirs.

Besides this, in order to shew my philosophy, I intend to find proper reflections upon every topick of the day. Reflections upon Ghosts, re-flections upon Black-friars bridge, and reflec-tions upon the Machine to carry Fish; in short, as I have nothing else to do, only let people make themselves ridiculous, and leave the rest to me.

For all this, as I said in the beginning, I ex-pect to be paid; and this I dare aver, that the reader will remember my advice, longer than I shall keep his money; for coin of all sizes has a surprizing facility of slipping from me. Let the reader then only permit me to eat, and I will endeavour to encrease his pleasures; his eatables and my philosophy will make a tolerable har-mony together. A rich Fool, and an *indigent Philosopher*, are made for each other's support; they fit like ball and socket: but this I insist on, that, if the Publick continue to keep me much longer in *indigence*, they shall see but very little more of my *philosophy*.

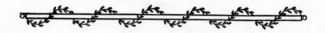

ESSAY XVI

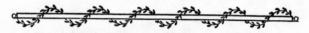

Numb. 2. The Author's Club[1]

Παντα γηλως.[2]

AS I was hunting last night for the topick of the day, after long search, I found myself quite out of luck. In mere despair, therefore, I went to my club at Cateaton, where I pass for a man of some humour in my way. As I make them laugh for nothing, they let me drink for nothing; or, to use the expression of the company, they never make any stranger of me.

This club, you ought to know, goes by the name of the Harmonical Society,[3] probably from that love of order and friendship which every person commends in institutions of this nature. The Landlord was himself our Founder. The

---

[1] From *Lloyd's Evening Post*, January 25–27, 1762.

[2] Probably a misprint for γἐλως.

[3] In revising his old essays for the collected edition of 1765, Goldsmith extracted the description of the Harmonical Society from this paper and inserted it into a paper on clubs originally published in the *Busy Body*, No. III, October 13, 1759 (see *Works*, I, 254–56). As he omitted certain portions of the description and made slight alterations in the others, I have thought it best to reprint the whole essay as it stands in *Lloyd's Evening Post*.

money spent is four-pence each, and we sometimes whip for a double reckoning. To this club
few recommendations are requisite, except the
introductory four-pence, and my Landlord's
good word, which, as he gains by it, he never
refuses. However, except myself, we have got no
very poor men amongst us; there is not a man
of them that could not shew four-pence at half
an hour's warning; and I know some who, by
proper address, could borrow half a crown among
their friends, with very little difficulty. Here
then I went to avoid the self-upbraidings to
which an indigent man is ever subject; to forget
that I was hungry, by resolving not to be a-dry;
and to drink to lose my appetite.

I found, as usual, the room filled with what
my Landlord below-stairs called very good company. There was neighbour Dibbens, that always disputes of religion; Ned Spungeit, that
never refused any man to be his three-halfpence;
Doctor Twist, that cures all manner of falling
sickness of long standing; Mr. Smokeum, that
cures all manner of beds and furniture of bugs
and vermin. These were of my acquaintance;
but there were twenty others that I never saw
before.

The reader may probably imagine that I am
going to give him the description of a new scene

of festivity, and introduce him to characters or manners that are able to divert or surprize. No, that has been anticipated by hundreds. We all here talked and behaved as every body else usually does on his club-night; we discussed the topick of the day, drank each others healths, snuffed the candles with our fingers, and filled our pipes from the same plate of tobacco. The company saluted each other in the common manner. Mr. Bellows-mender hoped Mr. Curry-comb-maker had not caught cold going home the last club-night; and he returned the compliment by hoping that young Master Bellows-mender had got well again of the lumps. Doctor Twist told us a story of a Parliament-man with whom he was intimately acquainted, while the Bug-man, at the same time, was telling a better story of a noble Lord with whom also he was intimately acquainted. A Gentleman, in a black wig and leather breeches, at t'other end of the table, was engaged in a long narrative of the Ghost in Cock-lane: He had read it in the Ledger, and was telling it to some that sate next him, who could not read. Near him Mr. Dibbens was disputing on the old subject of religion with a moral Philosopher, a Jew Pedlar, over the table, while the President vainly knocked down Mr. Leathersides for a song. Besides the combinations of these voices, which I could hear all together, and which formed an upper part to the concert, there were several others playing under-parts by themselves, and endeavouring to gain some luckless neighbour's ear, who was himself bent upon the same design against another.

We have often heard of the speech of a corporation, and this induced me to transcribe a speech of our club, taken in shorthand, word for word, as it was spoken last night by every member of the company. It may be necessary to observe, that the man who told of the Ghost, had the loudest voice, and the longest story to tell, so that his continuing narrative filled every chasm in the conversation.

"So, Sir, d'ye perceive me, the Ghost giving three loud raps at the bed-post—Says my Lord to me, my Dear Smokeum, you know there is no man upon the face of the yearth for whom I have so high—A damnable false heretical opinion of all sound doctrine and good learning; for I'll tell it aloud and spare not that.—Silence for a song; Mr. Leathersides, for a song—*As I was a walking upon the highway, I met a young damsel* —Then what brings you here, says the Parson to the Ghost—Sanconiathan, Manetho, and Berosus—The whole way from Islington turn-pike to Dog-house-bar—Dam—As for Abel

Drugger, Sir, he's damn'd low in it, my Prentice
boy has more of the Gentleman than he—For
murder will out one time or another; and none
but a Ghost, you know, Gentlemen, can—
Dammee if I don't, for my friend, whom you
know, Gentlemen, and who is a Parliament man,
a man of consequence, a dear, honest creature,
to be sure; we were laughing last night at—
Death and damnation upon all his posterity by
simply barely tasting.—Sour grapes, as the fox
said once when he could not reach them, and
I'll, I'll tell you a story about that that will make
you burst your sides with laughing; A fox once
—Will no body listen to the song—*As I was a
walking upon the highway, I met a young damsel
both buxom and gay*—No Ghost, Gentlemen, can
be murdered, nor did I ever hear but of one
Ghost killed in all my life, and that was stabbed
in the belly with a—My blood and soul, if I
do'nt—Mr. Bellows-mender, I have the honour
of drinking your very good health—Blast me if
I do—dam—blood—bugs—fire—whizz—blid—
tit—rat—trip—" The rest all riot, nonsense, and
rapid confusion.

Were I to be angry at men for being fools, I
could here find ample room for declamation;
but, alas! I have been a fool myself, and why
should I be angry with them for being something

so natural to every child of humanity. Go to
your clubs, ye honest tradesmen, and enjoy two
happy hours in the four and twenty. Yes, let us
drink porter, and eat sprats, for to-morrow we
die! And now sprats remind me of supper.
Reader go home and sup when you will, I'll go
home and sup when I can.

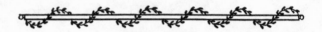

ESSAY XVII

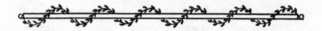

Onerat discentem turba; non instruit.[2]

SOME nights ago I was agreeably entertained with that part of Doctor Smollet's History of England, in which he characterizes the Writers and the Literature of the present times.[3] His style is rapid and elegant, and he is perhaps the first who ever undertook to dress the new-born occurrences of the day in the pompous robe of history. I was not a little mortified, however, to find that most of the Writers he mentions, as doing honour to the present age, are Scotchmen; and I am the more uneasy at this seeming partiality, as I am informed that Doctor Smollet is himself a native of Cornwall.

However this be, he has pretty largely expatiated upon names and abilities that posterity

[1] From *Lloyd's Evening Post*, January 29–February 1, 1762.

[2] Seneca *Dialogi* ix. 9. 4.

[3] See Smollett, *Continuation of the Complete History of England*, IV (1768), 125–30. This volume originally appeared in 1762.

may wish to know; yet still he has passed in silence the merit of many who deserve to be known. Mr. Henderson and Henriques, for instance, might have made some figure in history; the one as a Writer of Tragedies, the other as a speculative Politician. Mr. Ben. Victor might lay claim to admiration, either as Box-keeper, Laureat, or Historian, and Secretary Lockman be talked of for his skill as well in Heroicks as Herrings.[1] I cannot therefore avoid adding this Paper as a further supplement to the supplement in question, and, with the dignity of an Historian, endeavour to do justice to the Taste, the Genius, and the Literature of the times, in which I have the honour to live.

"In the early part of this reign the republic of letters began to put on a very flourishing appearance. In less than twelve revolutions of the moon the phœnix of taste seemed to revive from its own ashes, and expand its gaudy beauties to the sun. Never was the publication of periodical works, calculated both for the head and the

[1] Goldsmith had ridiculed this same group of persons a little less than a year before. See *Citizen of the World*, Letter CX (May 1, 1761): "I communicated this proposal some days ago in a company of the first distinction, and enjoying the most honourable offices of the state. Among the number were the Inspector of Great Britain, Mr. Henriques the director of the ministry, Ben. Victor the treasurer, John Lockman the secretary [this name was added in the collected edition of 1762], and the conductor of the Imperial Magazine." There are articles on Henderson, Victor, and Lockman in the *D.N.B.* See also Gibbs's notes in *Works*, III, 397.

heart, so frequent before; more than ten agreeable Magazines in a month, came flying all
abroad fraught with instruction and entertainment. The Gentleman's Magazine, remarkable
for its gravity and age. The London Magazine,
judiciously compiled from compilations; the
Universal Magazine, fricasseed from Diction-
aries; the Royal Magazine, written by a Society
of Gentlemen; the Imperial Magazine, calculated for the improvement of physick, and replete with a new system of anatomy; the sensible
British Magazine, the orthodox Christian's
Magazine; the Lady's Magazine, by a Lady of
very high quality; the Library Magazine; and
last, not least, that sly rogue the Court Magazine, dedicated to the Queen, enriched with her
face, and made up by Gentlemen of conspicuous
abilities and undoubted veracity. This was a fine
picture of the state of genius at that time; no
pert ribaldry through the whole; all serious,
chaste, temperate compilations, calculated to instruct mankind in the changes of the weather,
and to amuse them with eastern tales, replete
with grave essays upon wit and humour, and
humourous essays upon the cultivation of mad-
der and hemp. The smallness of the type, however, shut out two classes of readers to whom
they might have been otherwise very service-

able, children learning to read, and old women who read with spectacles.

"Nor while the arts of writing were cultivated, was the noble art of speaking forgotten. Eloquence was ever reckoned a divine art, and none but divine men were permitted to teach. As Paracelsus attempted to cure all disorders with opium, so a celebrated Orator of the times proposed to effect all things by eloquence.[1] From the government of a kingdom, to the dressing of a sallad, he insisted that eloquence could do it all. He taught mankind the mystery of declaiming poetry like prose, and reading prose like poetry. Cheesemongers were instructed to lay the proper emphasis upon *cheese;* and Taylors, taught by him, begged to take measure in measured periods.

In the same manner also the laurel crown in both kingdoms was placed upon deserving brows. The Odes of the English Laureat were finely solemn, and adumbrated with a mystic obscurity. The Odes of the Irish Laureat, though more familiar, were perhaps better adapted to the gay stupidity of a Court. An heroic poem also made its appearance at this time, pre-

---

[1] No doubt Thomas Sheridan, who in his *British Education: or, The Source of the Disorders of Great Britain* (1756) traced the major evils of contemporary society to the neglect of oratory. Goldsmith had discussed his claim in the *Bee,* No. VI, November 10, 1759 (*Works,* II, 407–8).

ferred by many Writers of News-papers and
Magazines, to Virgil and Homer; and justly too,
for poetry now was nothing else but a mosaic of
luxurious colours, cemented with a proper quantity of rash and inadequate epithets.[1] English
Pindarics now also were made to over-top the
obscurity of Pindar; and English Tragedies were
adapted only to Grecian readers.[2] At this time
also the renowned Chevalier Taylor,[3] Ophthal-
miater Pontifical Royal, published his own celebrated history, in which—but now I am men-
tioning the Chevalier Taylor, and Pindaric Odes,
I shall beg to step down from the stool of history,
for a moment, in order to present the Chevalier
with a blank Pindaric Ode in his praise, of my
own making; consisting of Strophe, Antistrophe,
Trochaics, Iambics, Sapphics, Pentameters,
Exameters, and a Chorus.

[1] Cf. Mr. Burchell's remark in chap. viii of *The Vicar of Wakefield:*
". . . . English poetry, like that in the latter empire of Rome, is nothing
at present but a combination of luxuriant images, without plot or connexion; a string of epithets that improve the sound, without carrying on
the sense." Goldsmith had made a similar criticism in *Citizen of the
World*, Letter XCVII (November 7, 1760).

[2] The latter part of this paragraph, including the parody of Gray's
Bard, implies views of poetry similar to those expressed by Goldsmith
in his review of Gray's *Odes* (*Works*, IV, 297–98) in his *Enquiry into the
Present State of Polite Learning* (*ibid.*, III, 513), and in his Dedication to
The Traveller (*ibid.*, II, 4).

[3] John Taylor (1703–72), oculist to George II. On the numerous
satires to which his bombastic pronouncements subjected him, see the
article in the *D.N.B.* His *History of the Travels and Adventures of the
Chevalier John Taylor, Opthalmiater* appeared in three volumes in 1761–62.

To the incomparable Chevalier Taylor,
A Pindaric Ode.

Strophe

Recitative, *accompanied.*

Perdition seize thee, shameless wight,
O blast thy eye-balls with eternal night;
May all the copper of thy forehead fail,
Thy bacon forehead smok'd in every jail.

Such were the sounds a Beldame once let fly,
The generous Taylor's needle quivering in her
eye.

Prithee woman do not ball,
Says gentle Taylor all the while,
I'll clap an artificial pupil.—

——We have room for no more.

ESSAY XVIII

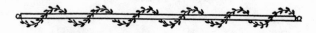

THE REVOLUTION IN LOW LIFE[1]

To the EDITOR *of* LLOYD'S EVENING POST.

SIR,

I SPENT part of the last summer in a little village, distant about fifty miles from town, consisting of near an hundred houses. It lay entirely out of the road of commerce, and was inhabited by a race of men who followed the primeval profession of agriculture for several generations. Though strangers to opulence, they

---

[1] From *Lloyd's Evening Post*, June 14–16, 1762; reprinted, in a truncated form, in the *Universal Museum, or Gentleman's and Ladies Polite Magazine*, I (June, 1762), 323–24, where it bears the title which I have adopted here.

The evidence for Goldsmith's authorship of this essay is mainly internal, but it could hardly, I believe, be more conclusive. The striking anticipation in the first half of the essay of the general situation treated eight years later in *The Deserted Village;* the harmony between the political views set forth in the second half and those expressed by Goldsmith on various occasions both before and after 1762; above all the precise parallels in idea and expression in both parts to passages in *The Traveller, The Vicar of Wakefield,* and *The Deserted Village*—these facts seem to me to lend themselves to only one explanation. We have seen, moreover, that Goldsmith had been almost certainly a contributor to *Lloyd's Evening Post* a few months before this essay appeared (see above, p. 98, n. 1), and we know that one of the owners of the paper was his chief employer at this time, John Newbery (cf. Charles Welsh, *A Bookseller of the Last Century* [London, 1885], pp. 161, 336). See the *Times Literary Supplement,* September 8, 1927, p. 607.

were unacquainted with distress; few of them were known either to acquire a fortune or to die in indigence. By a long intercourse and frequent intermarriages they were all become in a manner one family; and, when the work of the day was done, spent the night agreeably in visits at each other's houses. Upon those occasions the poor traveller and stranger were always welcome; and they kept up the stated days of festivity with the strictest observance. They were merry at Christmas and mournful in Lent, got drunk on St. George's-day, and religiously cracked nuts on Michaelmas-eve.[1]

Upon my first arrival I felt a secret pleasure in observing this happy community. The chearfulness of the old, and the blooming beauty of the young, was no disagreeable change to one like me, whose whole life had been spent in

[1] There is a striking similarity between this passage and the opening of chap. iv in *The Vicar of Wakefield:* "The place of our new retreat was in a little neighbourhood, consisting of farmers, who tilled their own grounds, and were equal strangers to opulence and poverty. As they had almost all the conveniencies of life within themselves, they seldom visited towns or cities in search of superfluity. Remote from the polite, they still retained a primæval simplicity of manners, and frugal by long habit, scarce knew that temperance was a virtue. They wrought with chearfulness on days of labour; but observed festivals as intervals of idleness and pleasure. They kept up the Christmas carol, sent true love-knots on Valentine morning, eat pancakes on Shrovetide, shewed their wit on the first of April, and religiously cracked nuts on Michaelmas eve" (text of the first edition, I [1766], 33–34). *The Vicar,* though not published until 1766, was probably in great part written by the summer of 1762 (see Charles Welsh, *A Bookseller of the Last Century,* pp. 58–59, and Alice C. C. Gaussen, *Percy: Prelate and Poet,* p. 144).

cities. But my satisfaction was soon repressed, when I understood that they were shortly to leave this abode of felicity, of which they and their ancestors had been in possession time immemorial, and that they had received orders to seek for a new habitation. I was informed that a Merchant of immense fortune in London, who had lately purchased the estate on which they lived, intended to lay the whole out in a seat of pleasure for himself.[1] I staid 'till the day on which they were compelled to remove, and own I never felt so sincere a concern before.

I was grieved to see a generous, virtuous race of men, who should be considered as the strength and the ornament of their country,[2] torn from their little habitations, and driven out to meet poverty and hardship among strangers. No longer to earn and enjoy the fruits of their la-

---

[1] Cf. the following account of the genesis of *The Deserted Village* given by an anonymous writer in the *Public Advertiser*, September 29, 1780: "We have already mentioned, that the Doctor occasionally retired into the country, and it was in rural stillness and solitude that he wrote The Deserted Village; where the poet pathetically deplores the depopulation of the country, and the disorders attendant on all the luxuries which commerce hath introduced. These did not all exist in his imagination only. In one of his country excursions he resided near the house of a great West Indian, in the neighbourhood of which several cottages were destroyed, in order to enlarge, or rather to polish, the prospect. This circumstance the Doctor often mentioned to evince the truth of his reasoning. . . . ."

[2] Cf. *The Deserted Village*, ll. 55–56:

> "But a bold peasantry, their country's pride,
> When once destroyed, can never be supplied."

bour, they were now going to toil as hirelings under some rigid Master, to flatter the opulent for a precarious meal, and to leave their children the inheritance of want and slavery. The modest matron followed her husband in tears, and often looked back at the little mansion where she had passed her life in innocence, and to which she was never more to return; while the beautiful daughter parted for ever from her Lover, who was now become too poor to maintain her as his wife.[1] All the connexions of kindred were now irreparably broken; their neat gardens and well cultivated fields were left to desolation.

[1] Cf. *The Traveller*, ll. 405-9:

> "Have we not seen at pleasure's lordly call,
> The smiling long-frequented village fall?
> Beheld the duteous son, the sire decay'd,
> The modest matron, and the blushing maid,
> Forc'd from their homes, a melancholy train, ... ?"

The same theme is developed in fuller detail in *The Deserted Village*, ll. 371-84 (I quote the text of the first edition):

> "The good old sire, the first prepared to go
> To new found worlds, and wept for others woe.
> But for himself, in conscious virtue brave,
> He only wished for worlds beyond the grave.
> His lovely daughter, lovlier in her tears,
> The fond companion of his helpless years,
> Silent went next, neglectful of her charms,
> And left a lover's for her father's arms.
> With louder plaints the mother spoke her woes,
> And blest the cot where every pleasure rose;
> And kist her thoughtless babes with many a tear,
> And claspt them close in sorrow doubly dear;
> Whilst her fond husband strove to lend relief
> In all the decent manliness of grief."

Strata jacent passim, hominumque
boumque labores.[1]

Such was their misery, and I could wish that
this were the only instance of such migrations of
late. But I am informed that nothing is at
present more common than such revolutions.[2]
In almost every part of the kingdom the laborious husbandman has been reduced, and the
lands are now either occupied by some general
undertaker, or turned into enclosures destined
for the purposes of amusement or luxury. Wherever the traveller turns, while he sees one part
of the inhabitants of the country becoming im-
mensely rich, he sees the other growing miserably poor, and the happy equality of condition
now entirely removed.[3]

[1] A combination of Virgil *Eclogues* vii. 54 and *Georgics* i. 118.

[2] Cf. the original form of ll. 405-6 of *The Traveller* as given in the
proof-sheets discovered by Bertram Dobell (now in the British Museum,
press-mark C. 58. g. 7):
"Have we not seen, at pleasure's lordly call,
An hundred villages in ruin fall?"
and the well-known passage in the Dedication of *The Deserted Village:*
". . . . I know you will object . . . . that the depopulation it deplores
is no where to be seen, and the disorders it laments are only to be found
in the poet's own imagination. To this I can scarce make any other
answer than that I sincerely believe what I have written; that I have
taken all possible pains, in my country excursions, for these four or five
years past, to be certain of what I alledge, and that all my views and
enquiries have led me to believe those miseries real, which I here attempt
to display."

[3] Cf. Goldsmith's discussion of the effects of the Marriage Act in
Citizen of the World, Letter LXXII (September 10, 1760): "An equal
diffusion of riches through any country ever constitutes its happiness.
. . . . How impolitic, therefore, are those laws which promote the accumu-

Let others felicitate their country upon the encrease of foreign commerce and the extension of our foreign conquests; but for my part, this new introduction of wealth gives me but very little satisfaction.[1] Foreign commerce, as it can be managed only by a few, tends proportionably to enrich only a few; neither moderate fortunes nor moderate abilities can carry it on; thus it tends rather to the accumulation of immense wealth in the hands of some, than to a diffusion of it among all; it is calculated rather to make individuals rich, than to make the aggregate happy.

Wherever we turn we shall find those governments that have pursued foreign commerce with too much assiduity at length becoming Aristocratical; and the immense property, thus necessarily acquired by some, has swallowed up the

---

lation of wealth among the rich; more impolitic still, in attempting to increase the depression on poverty!" See also his *History of England in a Series of Letters*, II (1764), 196–97.

[1] Cf. Goldsmith's answer in *Citizen of the World*, Letter XXV (April 1, 1760), to the politician who argued that "we are a commercial nation; we have only to cultivate commerce, like our neighbours the Dutch; it is our business to increase trade by settling new colonies; riches are the strength of a nation . . . ."; and *The Deserted Village*, ll. 269–73 (text of the first edition):

> "Proud swells the tide with loads of freighted ore,
> And shouting Folly hails them from her shore;
> Hoards, even beyond the miser's wish abound,
> And rich men flock from all the world around.
> Yet count our gains."

liberties of all. Venice, Genoa, and Holland, are little better at present than retreats for tyrants and prisons for slaves.[1] The Great, indeed, boast of their liberties there, and they have liberty. The poor boast of liberty too; but, alas, they groan under the most rigorous oppression.

A country, thus parcelled out among the rich alone, is of all others the most miserable. The Great, in themselves, perhaps, are not so bad as they are generally represented; but I have almost ever found the dependents and favourites of the Great, strangers to every sentiment of

---

[1] The theme of this and the latter part of the preceding paragraph is developed, in very similar language, in the long discourse of Dr. Primrose in chap. xix of *The Vicar of Wakefield:* "But an accumulation of wealth must necessarily be the consequence in a state when more riches flow in from external commerce, than arise from internal industry: for external commerce can only be managed to advantage by the rich, and they have also at the same time all the emoluments arising from internal industry: so that the rich, in such a state, have two sources of wealth, whereas the poor have but one. Thus wealth in all commercial states is found to accumulate, and such have hitherto in time become aristocratical. . . . . What they may then expect, may be seen by turning our eyes to Holland, Genoa, or Venice, where the laws govern the poor, and the rich govern the law" (text of the first edition, I, 202–6).

The phrase applied in the essay to Venice, Genoa, and Holland— "retreats for tyrants and prisons for slaves"—has a close parallel in l. 309 of *The Traveller,* in which Holland is described as "A land of tyrants, and a den of slaves." The formula had been in Goldsmith's mind since early in 1760, when he used it of the modern Persians in *Citizen of the World,* Letter XXXV (May 12, 1760): "A nation famous for setting the world an example of freedom, is now become a land of tyrants, and a den of slaves." Its source was possibly a passage in the *Literary Magazine* for 1756 (I, 4), in which Jamaica is characterized as "a place of great wealth and dreadful wickedness, a den of tyrants, and a dungeon of slaves." See the *Times Literary Supplement,* May 18, 1922, p. 324.

honour and generosity. Wretches, who, by giving up their own dignity to those above them, insolently exact the same tribute from those below. A country, therefore, where the inhabitants are thus divided into the very rich and very poor, is, indeed, of all others the most helpless; without courage and without strength; neither enjoying peace within itself, and, after a time, unable to resist foreign invasion.[1]

I shall conclude this paper with a picture of Italy just before its conquest, by Theodoric the Ostrogoth. "The whole country was at that time (says the Historian) one garden of pleasure; the seats of the great men of Rome covered the face of the whole kingdom; and even their villas were supplied with provisions not of their own growth, but produced in distant countries, where they were more industrious. But in proportion as Italy was then beautiful, and its possessors rich, it was also weak and defenceless. The rough peasant and hardy husbandman had been long obliged to seek for liberty and subsistence in Britain or Gaul; and, by leaving their native country, brought with them all the strength of the nation. There was none now to resist an

---

[1] Cf. Goldsmith's account of the fate of the Kingdom of Lao in *Citizen of the World*, Letter XXV (April 1, 1760), and *The Deserted Village*, ll. 265-86.

invading army, but the slaves of the nobility or the effeminate citizens of Rome, the one without motive, the other without strength to make any opposition. They were easily, therefore, over-come, by a people more savage indeed, but far more brave than they."

APPENDIX

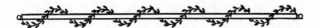

A S A basis for future research I venture to list
here a number of hitherto-unnoted essays and
other contributions to periodicals which seem to me
to exhibit more or less distinct traces of Goldsmith's
hand, but which, because of the meagerness of the
evidence, have necessarily been excluded from the
present collection. For most of them the final decision as to their authenticity will doubtless have to
await the elaboration of more precise methods of
stylistic analysis than have so far been applied to
questions of this kind. I group them under the titles
of the periodicals in which they appeared; in all cases
but one, it will be noted, these are periodicals for
which Goldsmith is known to have written during
the years in question.

The Busy Body

Four contributions by Goldsmith to this paper
have been identified. Two of them are poems—"The
Logicians Refuted" in No. V (October 18, 1759) and
"On the Taking of Quebec" in No. VII (October 22).
The other two are essays—a description of various
London clubs in No. III (October 13), later reprinted
in the *Essays* of 1765,[1] and an account of the popular

[1] See *Works* (ed. Gibbs), I, 249-59.

rejoicings over the recent victories in America in No. VI (October 20).[1] "Whatever other papers he may have furnished," wrote Prior, who was the first to discuss the question in detail, "are unknown, nor does internal evidence supply a clew to the discovery."[2]

Two other possibilities, however, should perhaps be considered. One is a paper in No. IV (October 16) describing humorously the Busy Body's experiences in French prisons. A passage toward the end reads as follows:

Happening one day to declare my sentiments pretty freely with regard to English liberty, and to rail at despotick power with a zeal which will undoubtedly meet with the approbation of every patriot, an *exempt* came up, and desired me *de par le roy*, to follow him. This summons was delivered in so polite a manner, that I could not avoid obeying it, and was immediately conducted to a hackney coach, which drove me to that celebrated mansion the Bastile, of which the ingenious Mons. de Voltaire, who had the honour of residing in it for some time himself, justly observes,

Il enferme souvent le crime et l'innocence.

As soon as the coach stopped I was led blind-fold through several windings and turnings, till I arrived at the cell allotted me as an apartment. . . . . I here saw amongst others . . . . the celebrated Abbé Freron, author of the *Journal Etranger*, but he was released in about a week. This gentleman in his periodical papers, takes such liberties with eminent persons, that he is frequently honoured with an apartment in this venerable mansion. I saw moreover the famous Chevalier D'Arc, author of *Mes Loisirs*,

---

[1] *Works*, IV., 462–68.   [2] *Life of Oliver Goldsmith*, I, 336.

and other miscellaneous pieces, who was imprisoned for having wrote certain verses, which gave offence to Madame de Pompadour.

The manner of this is clearly not unlike Goldsmith's. I should not press the point, however, were it not that the three French writers alluded to in the passage had all been mentioned a few months earlier in his *Enquiry into the Present State of Polite Learning*[1] and that Voltaire's residence in the Bastile had been described about the same time in his "Memoirs of M. de Voltaire."[2]

The other possibility is an essay entitled "The Flat-Bottomed Boats. A Vision" in No. VIII (October 25). The reference in the following passage to Goldsmith's description in No. VI of the popular rejoicings over the late victories may perhaps be interpreted as an indication of common authorship:

AFTER the little excursion mentioned in my last Paper, I returned home full of those patriot thoughts with which I concluded that Essay. When I had got within doors, the first thing that called my attention was the depredation, which puerile triumph had made on my peruke. Finding that I had lost only one of my ties in honour of the conquests of my country, I consoled myself with a retrospective view of the sufferings which others of my countrymen must have undergone in climbing inaccessible ascents, in opposing almost insurmountable difficulties, and in wresting by the hands of violence, the only place of strength which the French had on the American continent.[3]

[1] *Works*, III, 494, 511. Cf. also III, 74.

[2] *Ibid.*, IV, 9–10. On the date of this text see *ibid.*, p. 2.

[3] The French project for invading England in small boats, which furnished the occasion for the essay, is alluded to by Goldsmith in *Citizen of the World*, Letter V (February 7, 1760).

The Lady's Magazine

Investigation of Goldsmith's share in this periodical, of which he is known to have been for a time at least the editor,[1] is hampered by the circumstance that the first eleven numbers (September, 1759–July, 1760) seem not to be accessible in any of the fifty or more British and American libraries to which I have applied.[2] Fortunately, however, it is possible to learn the titles of the articles contained in these issues from contemporary advertisements and from reprints in other magazines, and this information, as will be seen, is not entirely without value. For the period between August, 1760, and the close of 1761, when Goldsmith's editorship would seem to have ended, the British Museum file is fairly complete.

1. Of the first eighteen numbers of the *Lady's Magazine*, no less than fifteen contain translations from the Spanish essayist, B. G. Feyjoo y Montenegro. The first of these, in the issue for September, 1759,[3] is a narrative entitled "The History of Villa Viciosa," the beginning of which is as follows:

At a small distance from Madrid is a little town, pleasantly situated and well built; but from the peculiar character of its first inhabitants distinguished by the reproachful name of Villa Viciosa. It is long since the occasion of its infamy has ceased; and various causes have been given for the name; for time devours truth; and conjecture after

---

[1] See above, p. xxxii, n. 2.

[2] Prior appears to have seen only two numbers (September and October, 1759) during this period. See his *Life of Oliver Goldsmith*, I, 338.

[3] It is reprinted in the October number of the *Grand Magazine of Magazines* (III, 248–50), whence comes the text quoted here.

awhile assumes the name of History. The truth is found
only in a small tract, the Work of that illustrious Frejo;
whose Theatre of Criticism, we wish so ardently and un-
successfully to see in an English habit.

Following this, in the number for January, 1760,
came "A Defence of Women, from the original Spanish of the celebrated Frejo; never attempted in English before,"[1] further instalments of which appeared
monthly until February, 1761.[2] Now, we know that
Goldsmith was familiar at this time with the name
of the author of the *Theatro critico* and interested in
his work; for he had mentioned him with approval
in *An Enquiry into the Present State of Polite Learning*,[3] and still more recently had devoted a short
article to him in the *Bee*.[4] The hypothesis is not un-
reasonable, then, that he was responsible, as editor
if not as translator,[5] for the prominent place which
Feyjoo occupied in the early numbers of the *Lady's
Magazine*.

2. Two articles, which I know only by title, in
the issue for June, 1760,[6] deal with themes in which

[1] See the advertisement of this number in the *Public Ledger*, January 31.

[2] With the second instalment the name of the author becomes
"Feyjoo."

[3] *Works*, III, 488.

[4] *Ibid.*, II, 360–61.

[5] There is no reason to suppose that he knew Spanish. A selection
from the *Theatro critico*, however, was accessible in a French translation
by Vaquette d'Hermilly—*Théâtre critique, ou Discours différents sur
toutes sortes de matières pour détruire les erreurs communes* ..., Paris, 1742–
43. 2 vols.

[6] See the advertisement of this issue in the *Public Ledger*, July 2.

Goldsmith was interested at this time and may, consequently, be his work. They are (1) "The Events of War, and the bad Consequences attending it"[1] and (2) "On the Independency of Genius, and the Spirit which becomes a public Writer."[2]

3. In the number for October, 1760 (II, 111–13), is a paper entitled "The Theatre," the intention and method of which are explained as follows in the opening paragraph:

> I call it the scale of the Tragedians and Comedians; it is modelled on the scale of Painters, by the famous Mr. De Piles: this manner of forming a judgment on painting, has been happily imitated by a physician of genius,[3] who applied it to our nation: after those two great men, I intend to try how far it may be applicable to acting.

There is nothing in the substance or style of this article which points positively to Goldsmith as its author, but if we turn to the *Lady's Magazine* for January, 1761 (II, 252–56), we discover in one of the essays in that number—we are still well within the period of Goldsmith's editorship—the following reference to it:

> As I once gave my fair readers a scale of actors which did not displease, I may now be permitted to give them one of the poets also, which is supposed to consist of twenty degrees for each column. . . . .

[1] Cf. *Citizen of the World*, Letter XVII (March 13, 1760), entitled in the collected edition of 1762 "Of the war now carried on between France and England, with its frivolous motives."

[2] Cf. *Works*, II, 374–76; III, 512.

[3] The allusion is to Akenside, whose "Ballance of Poets" had appeared in Dodsley's *Museum*, II (1746), 165–69.

Then follows an essay which had appeared originally in the *Literary Magazine* for January, 1758 (III, 6–8), under the title of "The Poetical Scale," and which Prior,[1] followed by Gibbs, who first reprinted it,[2] ascribed with comparatively little hesitation to Goldsmith. If this attribution can be accepted—and the reappearance of the essay in the *Lady's Magazine* at a time when Goldsmith as editor was constantly filling its pages with reprints of pieces which he had originally published elsewhere[3] is at least a partial confirmation—then a certain presumption is established that he was also the author of the "scale of actors" in the October number.

4. This same number contains a short sketch entitled "A Lady of Fashion in the Times of ANNA BULLEN compared with one of modern Times" (II, 124–26), the concluding paragraphs of which seem to me quite in Goldsmith's manner. I may add that the first of these paragraphs parallels fairly closely in sentiment the opening of the essay on happiness in the *Bee*,[4] and that the second contains an interesting anticipation of lines 251–64 of *The Deserted Village*:

This was the whole course of a country life, with some few variations as to winter and summer, and we see even by this account that our ancestors had their agreeable methods of passing time as well as we. Refinement in

---

[1] *Life*, I, 232–36.   [2] *Works*, IV, 417–23.

[3] There are such reprints in the numbers for October, 1759; September, November, and December, 1760; January, April, May, and September, 1761; and January, 1762. See Prior, *Life*, I, 338, 365. Prior's list, however, is incomplete.

[4] See *Works*, II, 334.

pleasure can but little contribute to make our time pleasing, and all the improvements which we have of late made in pleasure, in reality amounts to no more than the bare changing one set of amusements for another. Our passions and our pride have been in all ages the same, but camelion like take a colour from the different objects that surround us. What pleases in an age of simplicity will be insipid when luxury prevails, as the passions become then so compounded that they assume a new form from that implanted by Nature, and must be gratified rather by artificial helps, than what Nature has to bestow.

Change brings us no nearer the good in view, than when we set out upon the journey. Artificial pleasure may amuse us for a moment, but the nearer Nature the longer every thing pleases, and as we recede from it we only make approaches to anxiety and discontent. The healthful morning repast, "The carol blythe beneath the greenwood tree;" the traveller's tale by the glimmering evening fire; the kiss snatched from ruddy health, have been the pleasures of every age, and will please for ever. The midnight masquerade, the prolonged brag party, the five hours labour of the toilet are only the pleasures of fashion and caprice, and will last no longer than till some more fashionable folly comes to take their place. Happy they who pursue pleasure as far as Nature directs, and no farther; pleasure rightly understood, and prudently followed, is but another name for virtue![1]

5. Besides the first instalment of Goldsmith's "Memoirs of M. de Voltaire," the *Lady's Magazine* for February, 1761, contains a long "Account of the Beaver, and their Houses on Beaver Creek in Hay's Island, Hudson's Bay" (II, 311–15). There is nothing in the body of the article that suggests Goldsmith's hand, but the first paragraph presents one of his favorite ideas:[2]

[1] *Lady's Magazine*, II, 125–26.   [2] See above, p. 26, n. 1.

Of all the animals endowed with sagacity, approaching that of man, the beaver is most remarkable. And this sagacity is greater in proportion, as men are less apt to intrude upon their little societies, a description therefore of that animal, and its sagacity will . . . . improve our knowledge in natural history.

6. Another possible contribution by Goldsmith is "The History of Mr. Regnard, the French Comic Poet" in the issue for July, 1761 (III, 28–32). The evidence is slight, but suggestive. In the first place, the substance of the essay—a rather romantic narrative of Regnard's travels and love-adventures—is derived in the main from the Introduction to a four-volume edition of the *Œuvres de M. Regnard*, published at Paris in 1758, and this edition, we know, was in Goldsmith's library at the time of his death.[1] In the second place, among the passages of the essay which have no counterpart in this Introduction is the following, in which the reader of Goldsmith will recognize one of the latter's favorite phrases:

Restless, anxious, and miserable, he could never remain for two days in the same place; he thus, like a philosophic vagabond,[2] travelled over all Europe, and went up to the desolate region of Lapland, 'till he was stopped by the frozen ocean.

The British Magazine

Although most of Goldsmith's fairly numerous essays in this magazine have doubtless been identi-

[1] See Prior, *Life*, II, 584.

[2] Goldsmith used the phrase in 1759 in No. I of the *Bee* (*Works*, II, 320) and again in the heading of chap. xx of *The Vicar of Wakefield* (probably written in 1761 and 1762).

fied, one or two possibilities yet remain to be considered.

1. In No. V of Vol. I (an extra number published between the regular issues for April and May, 1760) is an article bearing the title, "A curious Incident, translated from the Spanish" (I, 253–56). In its main substance it is merely another translation from Feyjoo's *Theatro critico*.[1] The Introduction, however, seems to be original and may be by Goldsmith, who, it will be remembered, was an active contributor to the *British Magazine* at this time,[2] and who had recently written of the skeptical tendencies of contemporary philosophers[3] and of the services of Feyjoo in disseminating modern ideas in Spain[4] in terms similar to those used here:

The connoisseurs of this age, who pique themselves upon their incredulity, have for some years employed the shafts of their ridicule upon the Norwegian bishop Pontoppidan, for seeming to adopt, in his natural history of Norway, certain extraordinary incidents relating to the wonders of the deep, some of which, according to his account, are indeed altogether astonishing. This may likewise be the fate of the following relation, translated from the Theatro Critico of that eminent author, Padre Feijoo, who hath enriched his native country by transplanting into it those discoveries of modern philosophy, to which, before his time, Spain was an utter stranger. It may not be amiss to observe, that his country has been grateful for the service he has done her, and that he has for some time been promoted to the dignity of a bishop.

[1] See above, p. 129.

[2] See above, p. xxxi.

[3] See *Works*, III, 496–97.   [4] See *ibid.*, II, 360–61.

2. A more interesting case is "The Distresses of an Hired Writer" in the issue for April, 1761 (II, 198–200). The general theme of this essay is "the crosses and disappointments which an author is liable to, merely as an author; . . . . most of which are . . . . owing to that fatal revolution whereby writing is converted to a mechanic trade; and booksellers, instead of the great, become the patrons and paymasters of men of genius." The subject is one which Goldsmith has already treated on several occasions— in *An Enquiry into the Present State of Polite Learning,*[1] in the *Bee,*[2] and in the *Citizen of the World.*[3] The title, moreover, recalls that of an essay which he had contributed to the *British Magazine* in June, 1760 (I, 369–72), and later reprinted as Letter CXIX in the collected edition of the *Citizen of the World* (1762) —"On the distresses of the poor exemplified in the life of a private centinel."[4] There are, besides, a few specific parallels to passages in various acknowledged works written before April, 1761. None of these, however, involves close verbal similarities, and it must be admitted that the total weight of the available evidence is not very great. The essay may be Goldsmith's, but decisive proofs are lacking, and in view of the fact that nothing that can be ascribed to him with any assurance had appeared in the *British*

[1] *Ibid.,* III, 503–4, 509.

[2] *Ibid.,* II, 444.

[3] See especially the end of Letter LXXXIV (October 17, 1760).

[4] The running head in the *British Magazine* is even closer: "The distresses of a common soldier."

Magazine since December, 1760, and that the views of the essayist on the harmful effects of the commercialization of literature were also shared by Smollett, who was editing the magazine at this time,[1] there is nothing to do but to suspend judgment until the evidence of style can be studied by means of more satisfactory tests than are now at our disposal.

The Public Ledger

1. In his notes on Goldsmith's "Memoirs of M. de Voltaire,"[2] Gibbs called attention to the fact that the translation given in that work of Voltaire's parallel between the English and French theaters[3] had previously appeared in the *Public Ledger* for November 12, 1760. I may add that two other translations included in the "Memoirs" as printed in the *Lady's Magazine* in 1761[4]—a letter from Frederick to Voltaire and Voltaire's reply, dated respectively August 8 and 26, 1736—had a similar history: they are to be found in the *Ledger* for August 27, 1760, prefaced by the following note:

As the Letter, from the King of Prussia to Mr. Voltaire in yours of Friday the 15th Instant was acceptable to the Publick, permit me to send you a Translation of two Letters more, which, as they have not hitherto appeared in our language, will, I hope give equal Entertainment and Instruction to your Readers.

[1] See *The Letters of Tobias Smollett, M.D.* (ed. E. S. Noyes; Cambridge, 1926), p. 68.

[2] *Works*, IV, 28, n. 2.

[3] *Ibid.*, pp. 28–30.

[4] III, 50–53 and 97–100. These translations are omitted from the modern reprints of Goldsmith's text.

If, as it seems reasonable to suppose, the author of
this note was Goldsmith, then it must have been he
who was responsible for the letter in the issue for
August 15 to which he refers in his opening clause.
This letter, which was not used in the "Memoirs,"
contains an invitation to Voltaire to come to Berlin;
it is thus introduced by the translator:

> As the minutest performances of great men are subjects
> of curiosity, as in them we often discover more of their real
> characters than in their actions performed in the eye of the
> world, permit me to send you a translation of one of the
> King of Prussia's letters to Mr. Voltaire; which, though
> only the result perhaps of indolence and familiarity, serves
> to give an idea of this great man's manner of amusing him-
> self with any friends in private.

2. Among the essays ascribed to Goldsmith in
1798, ostensibly on the authority of Thomas Wright,[1]
was a brief paper inspired by the preparations for the
approaching coronation of George III.[2] Though it
has usually been assumed that this essay was first
published in the December, 1760, number of the
British Magazine (I, 703-4), in reality it originally
appeared in the *Public Ledger* for December 9, 1760,
where it formed the second of a series of three papers
collectively entitled "The Weekly Correspondent."
The other two papers, published on December 2 and
16, dealt respectively with the reasons why the author was unwilling to reveal himself fully to his

[1] See above, pp. xiii–xiv.

[2] *Essays and Criticisms by Dr. Goldsmith*, III, 47–49. It was later
reprinted by Prior (*Miscellaneous Works*, I, 239–41) and by Cunningham
(*Works*, III, 286–87).

public and with the character of Tom Stucco, "a great lover of Building and Demolishing." The whole series was evidently the work of one writer, and there is some slight warrant, apart from the inclusion of the second essay in Wright's collection, for supposing that this writer was Goldsmith. His *Chinese Letters* were running in the *Ledger* at the time, though with diminishing frequency.[1] Moreover, though verbal parallels between the three essays and his acknowledged works are lacking, it is possible to see traces of his characteristic thinking in such a passage as the following from No. II:

> I am far from desiring to repress Curiosity, to which we owe so great a part of our intellectual pleasures;[2] nor am I hardy enough to oppose the general practice of mankind, so much as to think all pomp and magnificence useless or ridiculous. But all passions have their limits, which they cannot exceed without putting our happiness in danger. . . . .[3]

These considerations, however, are not decisive, and until further evidence can be discovered, the authorship of the series must remain uncertain.

The Royal Magazine

The signature "H. D.," which is appended to three out of the four articles reprinted above from this magazine (Essays III–V), recurs at the end of

[1] During December only three letters appeared, as contrasted with six in November and ten in October. See H. J. Smith, *Oliver Goldsmith's "The Citizen of the World"* (New Haven, 1926), p. 127.

[2] Cf. *Works*, III, 307.

[3] Cf. *ibid.*, II, 5, 9.

another short paper in the issue for February, 1761
(IV, 87–88). The subject—the present state of Russia and France—links the essay in a general way with
*The Political View of the Result of the Present War
with America* which Goldsmith was compiling about
this time.[1] The style, as will appear from the following extract, is fairly characteristic:

Let us now turn our eyes towards France, and consider
the state to which she is reduced by this long and expensive
war. It is well known that the inhabitants of that country,
have long flattered themselves with being some time or
other the arbiters of Europe: this chimerical notion, so
fatal to their peace, directed all their councils, and induced
them to be guilty of a thousand perfidies. But experience
has now convinced them, that what they had so long desired was impossible to be obtained; and that by grasping
at a shadow, they lost the substance. The consequence of
which is, that they now prefer the sickle to the sword, and
the ploughshare to any instrument of war. But what avails
their seeing their interest, if they are not at liberty to
pursue it? Their great ones are deaf to the calls of humanity; and seem resolved, that their once flourishing country
shall be ruined. Every means of acquiring subsistence to
the poor is cut off; the recruiting serjeants are birds of prey,
who seize on the helpless husbandman; their fields are un-
tilled, and their vintage neglected; these useful offices are
committed to men, too aged either for the field of Mars, or
those of Ceres, or to women unacquainted with every
branch of agriculture. This is a true picture of the country:
in cities it is no better; their artificers are carried off to
fatten the great Germanic cemetery; those who remain
resemble owls, not daring to follow their employments by
day; provisions are extremely scarce throughout the kingdom; and if they were plentier, no money to purchase them.
What can their enemies wish more?

[1] See above, p. 91, n. 1.

The Christian's Magazine

I know of no positive evidence that Goldsmith wrote for this magazine.¹ Prior assumes that he did, and says that his receipts to Newbery for sums paid for translating "The Life of Christ" and "The Lives of the Fathers" have reference to articles originally printed in the *Christian's Magazine*.² He also implies, though his statement is somewhat confused, that a series of short biographies of the philosophers from Goldsmith's pen appeared in its pages at a somewhat later date.³ It is not clear, however, that Prior had ever seen a file of this periodical. Otherwise, he could scarcely have thought that one of Goldsmith's contributions was a life of Christ, for no such life is to be found in the seven volumes and one number which make up the British Museum set. On the other hand, there is a series of articles which may have been the "Lives of the Fathers" referred to in Goldsmith's receipts and another series which may be identical with the lives of the philosophers.

The first series ran somewhat irregularly from June, 1760, to December, 1764, and included brief biographies of St. Chrysostom (I, 54–67), St. Polycarp (I, 197–206), St. Cyprian (II, 203–11), St. Ambrose (II, 454–66), St. Augustine (III, 4–12, 51–60), St. Basil (III, 196–207), St. Ephraim (III, 339–43),

¹ The first number is dated May, 1760; the last number in the British Museum set, January, 1767. The publishers were J. Newbery and J. Coote.

² *Life*, I, 409–13, 479–80, 488.

³ *Ibid.*, II, 102.

St. Gregory Nazianzen (III, 531–40), St. Ignatius (IV, 99–105), Justin Martyr (IV, 291–97), St. Athanasius (V, 532–40), and a number of others.

The series on the philosophers began later, and included, after a short sketch of Pierre Bayle, signed "G," in the number for July, 1762 (III, 293–95), biographies of Herman Boerhaave (IV, 51–64, 105–6), John Swammerdam (V, 148–53), Hugo Grotius (VI, 195–205, 243–51), John Locke (VI, 484–95), Samuel Pufendorf (VII, 4–12), and Jacques Abbadie (VII, 228–32).

Goldsmith may have been responsible for some, though probably not for all, of these contributions. I know, however, of no certain means of identification.

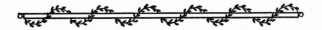

INDEX

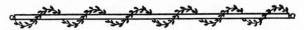